SPECTRUM®

Word Problems
Grade 6

Spectrum®

An imprint of Carson-Dellosa Publishing LLC
Greensboro, North Carolina

Spectrum® is an imprint of Carson-Dellosa Publishing.

Printed in the United States of America. All rights reserved. Except as permitted under the United States Copyright Act, no part of this publication may be reproduced or distributed in any form or by any means, or stored in a database or retrieval system, without prior written permission from the publisher, unless otherwise indicated. Spectrum® is an imprint of Carson-Dellosa Publishing. © 2014 Carson-Dellosa Publishing.

Send all inquiries to:
Carson-Dellosa Publishing
P.O. Box 35665
Greensboro, NC 27425 USA

Printed in the USA   ISBN 978-1-62442-732-9

04-284167811

Table of Contents Grade 6

Table of Contents, continued

Check What You Know

Adding and Subtracting through 6 Digits

Read the problem carefully and solve. Show your work under each question.

A traffic engineering company performed a survey of the vehicles using a section of a highway. During the survey period, the engineers counted 34,780 cars, 12,679 small commercial vehicles, 2,410 medium trucks, 14,397 large trucks, and 876 other vehicles.

1. What is the total number of medium and large trucks that used the highway during the survey?

_____16,807_____ trucks

14,397
2,410
16,807

2. Out of all the vehicles classified as other vehicles, 664 of them were motorcycles. How many of the other vehicles were not motorcycles?

___212___ were not motorcycles

3. How many of the vehicles that were counted in the survey were not classified as cars?

___30,362___ vehicles were not cars

16,807
12,679
29,486

4. About how many small commercial vehicles and medium trucks used the highway during the survey?

about ___15,000___ commercial vehicles and medium trucks

5. What is the difference between the number of large trucks and the number of medium trucks counted in the survey?

___11,987___ trucks

6. What is the total number of vehicles that passed the survey point during the counting period?

___65,142___ vehicles

29,486
+ 876
30,362

Lesson 1.1 Adding and Subtracting 2 and 3 Digits

Read the problem carefully and solve. Show your work under each question.

Lee bought a bag of 500 marbles. He sorted the marbles by color. He had 163 red marbles, 175 green marbles, 98 yellow marbles, and 64 blue marbles.

Helpful Hint

When two digits add up to more than 10, rename the digits and carry, if necessary. For example:

```
    1
    1 8
 +  1 9
 _____
    3 7
```

17 is renamed as 1 ten and 7 ones.

1. Lee placed all of the red marbles and the yellow marbles in one bag. How many marbles were in the bag in total?

   _____261_____ marbles

2. Lee placed the blue and green marbles in another bag. How many marbles altogether were in that bag?

   _____239_____ marbles

3. Of the 500 marbles, how many were not green?

   _____325_____ marbles

4. There were two sizes of red marbles. If 18 of the red marbles were large, how many small red marbles were in the bag?

   _____145_____ red marbles

5. If Lee gave 128 of the marbles to his friend Anna, how many marbles did he still have?

   _____372_____ marbles

Lesson 1.2 Adding and Subtracting Large Numbers and Estimating

Read the problem carefully and solve. Show your work under each question.

Taro is researching the population of Alaska. He finds that the largest cities in Alaska are Anchorage, Fairbanks, and Juneau. He learns that in 2006, the population of Anchorage was 278,700 people. The city of Fairbanks had a population of 31,142 people, and Juneau had a population of 30,737 people.

Helpful Hint

To estimate a sum or difference, round each number to the highest place value they have in common, and then add or subtract.

If the digit to the right of the place value is equal to or greater than 5, round to the next higher number.

1. In 2006, about how many people lived in Fairbanks and Juneau combined?

about ___6,879___ people

2. In 2006, about how many people lived in Anchorage and Juneau combined?

about ___310,000___ people

3. Based on the 2006 census, what was the exact population of Anchorage and Juneau combined?

___309,437___ people

4. If the total population of Alaska in 2006 was 670,053, how many people in Alaska did not live in Anchorage?

___391,353___ people

5. If 5,350 visitors came to Juneau for a festival in 2006, about how many people were in the city during the festival?

about ___36,800___ people

Lesson 1.3 Adding 3 or More Numbers (3 through 6 digits)

Read the problem carefully and solve. Show your work under each question.

There are five CD stores in an area. The chart below shows the number of CDs sold at each store in January.

Store A	Store B	Store C	Store D	Store E
4,569	8,822	16,725	6,224	42,480

Helpful Hint

When adding numbers with different amounts of digits, be sure to line the numbers up correctly by place value before adding.

1. Store A, Store B, and Store C are owned by the same company. How many CDs altogether did that company sell in January?

   ~~30,116~~ CDs

   30,116

2. Store B, Store C, and Store D are located in the same shopping center. How many CDs were sold in that shopping center in all?

   31,771 CDs

3. All of the sales at Store E were made online and all of the sales at the other stores were made in person. How many of the CDs were sold in person?

   36,340 CDs

4. In addition to CDs, Store E sells t-shirts and posters. If there were 1,219 t-shirts and 367 posters sold in January, what was the total number of products sold by Store E during this month?

   ~~44,066~~ products

   44,066

5. How many CDs altogether were sold at the area stores in January?

   78,820 CDs

Check What You Learned

Adding and Subtracting through 6 Digits

Read the problem carefully and solve. Show your work under each question.

Students from the middle schools in the city collected pennies for a charity fundraising event. The table below shows the number of pennies collected at each school.

School	Eastwood	Central	Highlands	Lincoln	Riverside
Pennies	958	14,657	32,287	4,321	32,116

1. What was the total number of pennies collected at Central and Lincoln?

   ____18,978____ pennies

4. About how many pennies altogether were collected by students at Central and Highlands?

   about ____40,000____ pennies

2. At Eastwood School, the sixth graders collected 561 pennies. How many pennies were collected by the other grades?

   ____397____ pennies

5. How many more pennies did the students at Riverside collect than the students at Central?

   ____17,459____ pennies

3. How many pennies were collected by schools other than Riverside?

   ____52,223____ pennies

6. How many pennies were collected by all of the schools combined?

   ____84,339____ pennies

Check What You Know

Multiplying and Dividing Whole Numbers

Read the problem carefully and solve. Show your work under each question.

Shawna will read 8 books during the summer. There are 2,325 total pages in her 8 books. Jake will read 7 books during the summer. There are 2,047 total pages in his 7 books. Shawna will read the same number of pages each day. Jake will also read the same number of pages each day.

1. There are 89 days of summer break. How many pages will Shawna read each day? How many pages will she have left?

_____26_____ pages   _____4_____ pages left

2. How many pages will Jake read each day during the 89 days of summer break? How many pages will he have left?

_____23_____ pages   _____0_____ pages left

3. One of Jake's books has 24 chapters. If each chapter has exactly 15 pages, how long is the book?

_____360_____ pages

4. Shawna reads 25 pages per hour. How many hours will she spend reading the 8 books?

_____93_____ hours

5. Jake reads 23 pages per hour. How many hours will he spend reading the 7 books?

_____89_____ hours

6. If each page has an average of 212 words, about how many words will Shawna read during the summer?

about _____492,900_____ words

Lesson 2.1 Multiplying 2, 3, and 4 Digits by 1 and 2 Digits

Read the problem carefully and solve. Show your work under each question.

A charter bus company owns 232 buses. Each bus can carry 42 passengers plus their luggage. The company also owns 28 vans. Each van can carry 13 passengers.

Helpful Hint

To multiply by a two-digit number, first multiply the top number by each of the digits in the bottom number. Then, add the two products to find the solution.

1. A school requests 6 buses for a field trip. How many passengers altogether can fit on 6 buses?

_____252_____ passengers

2. What is the maximum number of passengers that could travel in the company's buses?

_____9,744_____ passengers

3. An after-school program needs 5 vans for a field trip. How many passengers in all can 5 vans hold?

_____65_____ passengers

4. On one particular trip, there are 38 passengers riding on a bus. If each passenger is allowed to bring 122 pounds of luggage, what is the most that the luggage could weigh?

_____4,636_____ pounds

5. What is the total number of passengers that could ride in the company's vans?

_____364_____ passengers

6. The company plans to purchase 4 new tires for each of its buses and vans. How many total tires will it need?

_____1,040_____ tires

Lesson 2.2 Multiplying 3 and 4 Digits by 3 Digits

Read the problem carefully and solve. Show your work under each question.

Peter starts a job at an electronics store. He learns that the image on a computer or television screen is made by lighting up small dots, called *pixels*, that are lined up in rows and columns. He can find the total number of pixels on a screen by multiplying the number of rows by the number of columns. Peter decides to investigate the total number of pixels on different equipment.

Helpful Hint

Remember to add zeros at the end of the second and third products to show that you are multiplying 433 by 2 tens and 3 hundreds:

```
        4 3 3
   ×    3 2 1
   ─────────
        4 3 3
      8 6 6 0
 + 1 2 9 9 0 0
 ─────────────
   1 3 8 9 9 3
```

1. Peter found a television screen that has 576 columns with 720 pixels in each column. How many pixels does this screen have?

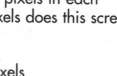 414,720 pixels

2. How many pixels are there on a computer screen that has 768 rows with 1,024 pixels in each row?

786,432 pixels

3. Peter learns that a digital camera uses pixels in rows and columns to make a photograph. How many pixels are there in a digital photograph that is 960 by 1,344 pixels?

1,290,340 pixels

Lesson 2.3 Dividing 2, 3, and 4 Digits by 1 Digit

Read the problem carefully and solve. Show your work under each question.

A small manufacturing company produces picture frames sold at craft stores. The frames are sold in packages containing 4, 5, or 8 frames per package.

Helpful Hint

Remember to write the first digit of the quotient in the correct spot.

$$\begin{array}{r} 58 \\ 6\overline{)348} \end{array}$$

Since $100 \times 6 = 600$ and 600 is greater than 348, there is no hundreds digit in the quotient.

1. During one hour at the factory, workers assembled 95 frames. If all the frames were placed in packages of 5 frames each, how many packages were produced? How many frames were left over?

_____19_____ packages

_____0_____ frames left

2. During one shift, the factory produced only packages containing 8 frames each. If the total number of frames was 730, how many full packages were assembled? How many frames were left over?

_____91_____ packages

_____2_____ frames left

3. The company received an order for 250 frames. The boss does not want any frames left over. How many frames should be in each package so there are no frames left over? How many packages will there be in total?

_____5_____ frames in a package

_____50_____ packages

4. For one order, the factory made frames for packages containing 4 frames each. If a total of 4,127 frames were built, how many full packages could be shipped? How many frames would be left?

_____1,031_____ packages

_____3_____ frames left

5. The company made 389 frames for another order. Each package needed to contain 8 frames. How many packages were produced? How many frames were left over?

_____48_____ packages

_____5_____ frames left

Lesson 2.4 Dividing 2 through 5 Digits by 2 Digits

Read the problem carefully and solve. Show your work under each question.

During a political campaign, volunteers call voters to give them information about a candidate. Each volunteer receives a list of names and phone numbers. The names are always divided evenly between all the volunteers.

Helpful Hint

When dividing, make sure the numbers are positioned correctly with each step:

$$\begin{array}{r} 19\ R1 \\ 17\overline{)324} \\ 17 \\ \hline 154 \\ 153 \\ \hline 1 \end{array}$$

1. On the first day of the campaign, 22 volunteers came to the call center. If there were 1,012 voters in the district, how many names were on each volunteer's list?

   _____46_____ names

2. Before any calls were made, 3 more volunteers came. The 1,012 voter names were divided again. How many names were on each volunteer's list? How many names were left?

   _____40_____ names

   _____12_____ names left

3. In the second week of the campaign, there were 58 volunteers. 13,075 voters were divided evenly among them. Their supervisor called the remaining people. How many calls did each volunteer make?

   _____225_____ calls

4. During the second week, the 58 volunteers called an additional 2,430 voters. Again, each volunteer called the same number of voters. Their supervisor called the remaining people. How many additional calls did each volunteer make that week?

   _____41_____ additional calls

5. On the day of the election, follow-up calls were made to 575 voters. If there were 18 volunteers in the office, how many calls did each person make? How many names were left?

   _____31_____ calls

   _____17_____ names left

Lesson 2.5 Estimating Products and Quotients

Read the problem carefully and solve. Show your work under each question.

A fuel distributor has three trucks that are used to deliver gasoline to stations. When filled, the trucks hold the amounts of fuel shown in the chart.

Truck 1	987 gallons
Truck 2	1,612 gallons
Truck 3	5,685 gallons

Helpful Hint

To estimate products, round each number to its highest place value and multiply.

To estimate quotients, round the dividend to a number that is easy to divide mentally.

1. On one round of deliveries, Truck 2 stops at 5 stations. If each station receives the same amount of gasoline, about how many gallons can be pumped at each station?

   about ____300____ gallons

2. There are about 4 liters in a gallon. About how many liters of gasoline can Truck 2 deliver in one load?

   about ___8,050___ liters

3. Several of the distributor's customers have tanks that hold only 90 gallons of gasoline. About how many of these tanks can be filled from Truck 3?

   about ___60___ tanks

4. The average sale at a station is 8 gallons per purchase. About how many sales can be made from one 490 gallon tank?

   about ___50___ sales

5. Truck 1 was emptied and refilled 129 times in one month. About how many total gallons of gas did Truck 1 deliver?

   about ___100,000___ gallons

Check What You Learned

Multiplying and Dividing Whole Numbers

Read the problem carefully and solve. Show your work under each question.

Seven schools participated in a health challenge. As part of the challenge, the students pledged to walk the same distance every day. In total, students walked 45,416 miles during the month-long challenge.

1. There were 31 days in the challenge. How many full miles did the students walk each day in total?

_____ full miles

2. What was the remainder when the number of miles walked each day was calculated?

_____

3. Leslie walked exactly 13 miles each day for the 31 days of the challenge. How many miles did Leslie walk in all?

_____ miles

4. Each school had 4 teams that participated in the health challenge, making a total of 28 teams. Each team had the same number of people. How many full miles did each team walk?

_____ full miles

5. The same number of students from each of the 7 schools participated in the challenge. About how many miles did the students at each school walk?

about _____ miles

6. Each mile walked took about 19 minutes. About how many total minutes did the students spend walking during the challenge?

about _____ minutes

Check What You Know

Understanding Fractions

Read the problem carefully and solve. Show your work under each question.

Lionel builds wooden furniture that he sells at his shop. This week, he plans to make 3 tables, 9 chairs, 15 stools, and 2 cabinets. After several days, he has completed $3\frac{7}{8}$ tables, $\frac{2}{3}$ of a chair, $13\frac{4}{14}$ stools, and $\frac{4}{5}$ of a cabinet.

1. Lionel looks at the numbers of each type of furniture he plans to make: 3, 9, 15, and 2. Which of these numbers are prime?

_____

2. Lionel compares the fractions that show how much of a chair and how much of a cabinet he has completed so far. Rename the pair of fractions so they have common denominators.

_____ and _____

3. How can the number of tables Lionel has completed be written as an improper fraction?

_____

4. Lionel wants to rewrite the number of stools he has completed. What is this mixed numeral in simplest form?

_____

5. How can the number of stools Lionel has completed be written as an improper fraction?

_____

6. Lionel wants to display the chairs and stools together in groups. Each display will have the same number of chairs and stools. What is the greatest common factor of 9 and 15?

_____

Lesson 3.1 Prime and Composite Numbers

Read the problem carefully and solve. Show your work under each question.

Lauren and her younger brother John compare their coins. They make the chart on the right, which shows the number of each type of coin they have.

	Lauren	John
Pennies	4	11
Nickels	13	9
Dimes	5	7
Quarters	8	15

Helpful Hint

A **prime number** is any number greater than 1 that has only two factors, itself and 1.

A **composite number** has more than two factors.

1. Lauren looks at the numbers of coins on the chart. She notices that both of the numbers listed next to one type of coin are prime numbers. What is that coin?

_____

2. Lauren also notices that one type of coin has only composite numbers listed on the chart. What is that coin?

_____

3. Lauren has a total of 30 coins. Use a factor tree to find the prime factorization of 30.

_____

4. Together, Lauren and John have 72 coins. Use a factor tree to find the prime factorization of 72.

_____

Lesson 3.2 Reducing Fractions to Their Simplest Form

Read the problem carefully and solve. Show your work under each question.

Kamala owns a flower shop. Today, she arranges flowers into vases. She has 12 roses, 8 tulips, 18 lilies, and 10 daffodils. Kamala has 3 different colored vases: red, blue, and green.

Helpful Hint

The **greatest common factor** is the largest number that can evenly divide into two or more numbers.

Example: Common factors of 18 and 24 are 2 and 6. The greatest common factor is 6.

1. Kamala arranges the roses and tulips together. She wants to put the same number of each flower in each vase, so she finds the greatest common factor of the number of roses and tulips. What is the greatest common factor of 12 and 8?

_____

2. Kamala wants to arrange the lilies and daffodils together. She finds the greatest common factor of the number of lilies and daffodils. What is the greatest common factor of 18 and 10?

_____

3. Kamala finds that $\frac{4}{18}$ of the lilies are wilted. What is this fraction written in its simplest form?

_____

4. $\frac{10}{48}$ of the total flowers are daffodils. What is this fraction written in its simplest form?

_____

5. Kamala decides to put all of her arrangements in blue vases. $\frac{4}{16}$ of her vases are blue. What is this fraction in its simplest form?

_____

Lesson 3.3 Finding Common Denominators

Read the problem carefully and solve. Show your work under each question.

Mr. Blanco is the coach of the track team. As part of practice, he has several runners sprint around the track. After a few minutes, Mr. Blanco has the runners stop and record their distance. Their distances, in fractions of a mile, are on the chart at the right.

Andy	$\frac{2}{3}$ mile
Eartha	$\frac{7}{10}$ mile
Jerome	$\frac{3}{5}$ mile
Sarah	$\frac{7}{12}$ mile

Helpful Hint

The **least common multiple** of two numbers is the smallest number that is a multiple of both.

1. Mr. Blanco wants to compare Andy and Jerome's distances. Rename their fractions with a common denominator.

_____ and _____

2. Mr. Blanco wants to compare Eartha and Jerome's distances. Rename their fractions with a common denominator.

_____ and _____

3. Sarah says that she ran farther than Jerome. Rename their fractions with a common denominator and compare using >, <, or =.

_____

4. What is the least common multiple of all four denominators in the chart?

_____

5. Use the least common multiple to compare all the runners' distances with a common denominator. Who ran the farthest?

_____

Lesson 3.4 Changing Improper Fractions to Mixed Numerals

Read the problem carefully and solve. Show your work under each question.

Chelsea is baking muffins for the school bake sale. To make her famous blueberry bran muffins, Chelsea makes a list of the ingredients she needs. This list includes $\frac{40}{3}$ cups of flour, $\frac{42}{5}$ cups of milk, $\frac{8}{3}$ cups of brown sugar, $\frac{50}{7}$ cups of blueberries, and $\frac{7}{4}$ teaspoons of ground cinnamon.

1. Change the amount of ground cinnamon Chelsea needs to a mixed numeral.

   _____ teaspoons

Helpful Hint

Compare two mixed numerals in the same way as a regular fraction, by finding a common denominator.

4. Chelsea buys a box of brown sugar that has $\frac{7}{3}$ cups of brown sugar. Change the amount she needs for the recipe into a mixed numeral. Did she buy enough brown sugar?

   _____ cups

   _____

2. Change the amount of milk that Chelsea needs into a mixed numeral.

   _____ cups

3. Change the amount of blueberries that Chelsea needs into a mixed numeral.

   _____ cups

5. Chelsea buys a bag of flour that has $\frac{45}{2}$ cups of flour. Change the amount of flour she needs into a mixed numeral. Did she buy enough flour?

   _____ cups

   _____

Lesson 3.5 Changing Mixed Numerals to Improper Fractions

Read the problem carefully and solve. Show your work under each question.

Chelsea also makes granola bars for the bake sale, so she writes a list of the ingredients she needs. Some of the ingredients on this list are $2\frac{1}{2}$ sticks of butter, $4\frac{2}{7}$ cups of raisins, $1\frac{1}{5}$ cups of sesame seeds, $2\frac{2}{3}$ cups of brown sugar, $4\frac{1}{3}$ cups of almonds, and $14\frac{1}{4}$ cups of oats.

Helpful Hint

To change a mixed numeral into a fraction:

1. Multiply the denominator by the whole number.
2. Add the numerator.
3. Put this number over the original denominator.

1. Change the amount of sesame seeds Chelsea needs to an improper fraction.

_____ cups

2. Change the amount of butter that Chelsea needs into an improper fraction.

_____ sticks

3. Change the amount of oats that Chelsea needs into an improper fraction.

_____ cups

4. Change the amount of raisins and almonds that Chelsea needs to improper fractions.

_____ cups of raisins

_____ cups of almonds

5. Does Chelsea need more raisins or almonds for her granola bar recipe? Explain your answer.

_____

_____

Lesson 3.6 Simplifying Mixed Numerals

Read the problem carefully and solve. Show your work under each question.

Benito volunteers at the local library. He made the chart on the right to show the number of hours he worked at the library each day last week.

Monday	$3\frac{8}{5}$ hours
Tuesday	$1\frac{15}{4}$ hours
Wednesday	$1\frac{7}{3}$ hours
Thursday	$1\frac{12}{8}$ hours
Friday	$3\frac{6}{8}$ hours

Helpful Hint

A mixed numeral is not in simplest form if:

1. The fraction is not reduced.
2. The fraction is improper.

1. Change the hours that Benito worked on Monday to a mixed numeral in its simplest form.

_____ hours

2. Change the hours that Benito worked on Tuesday to a mixed numeral in its simplest form.

_____ hours

3. Change the hours that Benito worked on Wednesday to a mixed numeral in its simplest form.

_____ hours

4. Benito added up the hours he worked on Thursday and Friday. What is this number in its simplest form?

_____ hours

5. Which day did Benito work the most?

_____

Check What You Learned

Understanding Fractions

Read the problem carefully and solve. Show your work under each question.

A group of teachers is helping Mr. Chen correct papers for his class. They have to correct 12 math tests, 9 book reports, 11 vocabulary quizzes, and 4 science tests. So far, they have corrected $5\frac{5}{6}$ math tests, $\frac{27}{5}$ book reports, $3\frac{19}{4}$ vocabulary quizzes, and $\frac{9}{12}$ of a science test.

1. Mr. Chen notices that one of the numbers of tests they have to correct is a prime number. What is that number?

_____

2. Ms. Canales wants to compare the number of corrected book reports and the number of corrected science tests. What is the least common denominator for these fractions?

_____

3. Ms. Jackson is correcting the science tests. How can $\frac{9}{12}$ be written in its simplest form?

_____

4. Ms. Ahn is correcting the math tests. How can the number of math tests that she has corrected so far be written as an improper fraction?

_____

5. Mr. Wood is correcting the vocabulary quizzes. How can the number of vocabulary quizzes that he has corrected so far be written as a mixed numeral in its simplest form?

_____

6. Change the number of vocabulary quizzes corrected so far into an improper fraction in its simplest form.

_____

Check What You Know

Adding and Subtracting Fractions

Read the problem carefully and solve. Show your work under each question.

Members of the soccer team meet every day at the park for practice. The chart below shows how far six members of the soccer team live from the park.

Ayame	Cindy	Della	Lita	Mandy	Susan
$\frac{7}{8}$ mile	$2\frac{2}{3}$ miles	$4\frac{2}{5}$ miles	$\frac{3}{8}$ mile	$5\frac{3}{7}$ miles	$\frac{3}{5}$ mile

1. Ayame and Lita both walk from their homes to the park. How much farther does Ayame walk?

_____ mile

2. After practice, Lita and Ayame go to Lita's house together. What total distance does Ayame walk from her house to the park and from the park to Lita's house?

_____ miles

3. How much farther does Susan live from the park than Lita?

_____ mile

4. Cindy and Della both ride their bicycles to practice. What is the combined distance of their houses to the park?

_____ miles

5. How much farther does Della ride her bicycle than Cindy?

_____ miles

6. Mandy lives the farthest from the park. How much farther away does she live from the park than Ayame?

_____ miles

Lesson 4.1 Adding and Subtracting with Unlike Denominators

Read the problem carefully and solve. Show your work under each question.

Rosa and Tom are in charge of the food for their grandmother's birthday party. They set out 2 pitchers of juice, 2 blocks of cheese, a box of crackers, and a large bowl of salad.

Helpful Hint

Rename fractions with the least common denominator and change to simplest form.

Example: $\frac{2}{3} + \frac{1}{2}$

$\frac{4}{6} + \frac{3}{6} = \frac{7}{6} = 1\frac{1}{6}$

---

1. Tom is serving juice. He serves $\frac{5}{8}$ of a pitcher. An hour later, he serves $\frac{3}{4}$ of the other pitcher. How much juice has he served in all?

_____ pitchers

2. Rosa checks to see how much of the cheese has been eaten. One block has $\frac{2}{3}$ left, and the other has $\frac{3}{4}$ left. How much cheese is left?

_____ blocks

3. After one hour, the box of crackers has $\frac{5}{6}$ left. Later, $\frac{1}{3}$ of the box of crackers is left. What is the difference between these fractions?

_____

4. The salad fills $\frac{9}{10}$ of a large bowl. Rosa serves some of the salad, and then $\frac{1}{5}$ of the bowl has salad. What is the difference between these fractions?

_____

5. After the party, Tom and Rosa share 2 bowls of leftover food. The first bowl is $\frac{2}{3}$ full of crackers, and the second bowl is $\frac{7}{10}$ filled with salad. How much total food do they share?

_____ bowls

Lesson 4.2 Adding Mixed Numerals with Unlike Denominators

Read the problem carefully and solve. Show your work under each question.

A group of sixth graders participate in a charity walkathon. People from the area have pledged money to the students. The farther they walk, the more money they raise. After an hour, Dylan has walked $2\frac{5}{6}$ miles, Meredith has walked $1\frac{5}{9}$ miles, Aida has walked $2\frac{1}{3}$ miles, Taci has walked $3\frac{1}{5}$ miles, and Ellis has walked $3\frac{1}{2}$ miles.

1. Ms. Hyoshi pledged money to both Aida and Dylan. How far altogether have Aida and Dylan walked?

   _____ miles

Helpful Hint

When adding three mixed numerals, rename the fractions so that all three have one common denominator. Remember to simplify the answer.

4. Mr. and Mrs. Gonzales have pledged money to Dylan, Meredith, and Ellis. How far have these 3 students walked?

   _____ miles

2. Mr. Franklin has pledged money to Aida and Ellis. How far have they walked in all?

   _____ miles

5. Ms. Gomez says that she will pledge money to the 3 students in the group who walk the farthest. What is the combined distance of these students?

   _____ miles

3. Mr. Agoyo, Taci's father, wants to know how far she and her friend Meredith have walked. What is this total?

   _____ miles

NAME_____

Lesson 4.3 Subtracting Mixed Numerals with Unlike Denominators

Read the problem carefully and solve. Show your work under each question.

After the charity walkathon, Dylan made the chart on the right. The chart shows the total distance each student walked. Dylan wants to use the chart to compare everyone's distances.

Aida	$8\frac{3}{4}$
Dylan	$7\frac{1}{2}$
Ellis	$9\frac{3}{5}$
Meredith	$6\frac{7}{12}$
Taci	$4\frac{1}{6}$

Helpful Hint

Rename if necessary. Simplify your answer.

$$4\frac{1}{4} \dashrightarrow 3\frac{5}{4}$$
$$-1\frac{3}{4} \dashrightarrow -1\frac{3}{4}$$
$$2\frac{2}{4} = 2\frac{1}{2}$$

3. How much farther did Ellis walk than Meredith?

_____ miles

1. How much farther did Aida walk than Dylan?

_____ miles

4. How much farther did Dylan walk than Meredith?

_____ mile

2. How much farther did Dylan walk than Taci?

_____ miles

5. How much longer did Ellis walk than Dylan?

_____ hours

Check What You Learned

Adding and Subtracting Fractions

Read the problem carefully and solve. Show your work under each question.

Francisco made a chart of the number of hours he studied each day this week.

Monday	Tuesday	Wednesday	Thursday	Friday
$\frac{2}{7}$ hour	$\frac{6}{7}$ hour	$3\frac{1}{6}$ hours	$2\frac{3}{4}$ hours	$1\frac{2}{3}$ hours

1. How long did Francisco study on Monday and Tuesday in total?

_____ hours

2. On Tuesday, Francisco studied math and science only. He studied math for $\frac{1}{2}$ hour. How long did he study science?

_____ hour

3. How long did Francisco study on Thursday and Friday in total?

_____ hours

4. On Wednesday, Francisco studied social studies and spelling only. He studied social studies for $1\frac{4}{5}$ hours. How long did he study spelling?

_____ hours

5. How many hours did Francisco study on Wednesday, Thursday, and Friday combined?

_____ hours

6. How much longer did Francisco study on Thursday than on Tuesday?

_____ hours

Check What You Know

Multiplying and Dividing Fractions

Read the problem carefully and solve. Show your work under each question.

Ms. Vega's class is planning a party to thank all the parents who helped their class during the year. The class spends time preparing for the party. The students want to make gifts for the parents. Many of them bring in supplies from home to make their gifts.

1. Before lunch, Mario and Sean painted $\frac{6}{8}$ of a thank-you banner. Sean painted $\frac{2}{3}$ of that amount. What part of the banner did Sean paint?

_____ of the banner

2. Cara brought in $\frac{6}{9}$ yard of blue ribbon to make her gift. She cuts the ribbon into 3 equal pieces. What is the length of each piece?

_____ yard

3. Inez brought in $\frac{7}{8}$ yard of red ribbon. She cuts the ribbon into equal pieces that are each $\frac{1}{5}$ yard long. How many pieces did she cut?

_____ pieces

4. Ms. Vega's class spends $\frac{3}{4}$ hour preparing for the party each day. How many hours do they spend in 4 days?

_____ hours

5. Chen brought in a $4\frac{1}{2}$-ounce bag of glitter but ran out. Cara brought in a bigger bag of glitter. Her bag is $1\frac{2}{3}$ times larger than Chen's bag. How many ounces is Cara's bag?

_____ ounces

6. Ms. Vega plans to bring in $4\frac{2}{5}$ pounds of fruit salad. She wants to divide it evenly between 4 bowls. How many pounds of fruit salad will be in each bowl?

_____ pounds

Lesson 5.1 Multiplying Fractions and Mixed Numbers by Whole Numbers

Read the problem carefully and solve. Show your work under each question.

Emily does a lot of activities during the week. Emily spends $\frac{3}{4}$ of an hour practicing piano every day. She also has basketball practice for $1\frac{2}{5}$ hours and spends $\frac{2}{3}$ of an hour walking her dog each day.

Helpful Hint

Before multiplying fractions and mixed numbers by whole numbers:

1. Rewrite the whole number as a fraction with 1 in the denominator.
2. Rename the mixed number as an improper fraction.

Remember to simplify all answers.

1. How many hours does Emily spend at basketball practice in 5 days?

_____ hours

2. Emily likes to walk her dog before she goes to school. How many hours does she walk her dog in 5 days?

_____ hours

3. How many hours does Emily practice the piano in 5 days?

_____ hours

4. During one week, the coach only held basketball practice for 3 days. How many hours did Emily have practice that week?

_____ hours

5. After basketball season is over, Emily plans to take an art class after school for 4 days each week. The class lasts for $1\frac{1}{4}$ hours each time. How many total hours will she have art class each week?

_____ hours

Lesson 5.2 Multiplying Mixed Numbers

Read the problem carefully and solve. Show your work under each question.

Gary's Garden Shop sells bags of grass seed, sand, and potting soil. The potting soil comes in small and large sizes. The grass seed and sand come in three different sizes: small, medium, and large.

Helpful Hint

Remember to rename each mixed numeral as an improper fraction before multiplying.

Be sure to simplify all fractions.

1. The small bag of potting soil weighs $3\frac{1}{4}$ pounds. The large bag weighs $3\frac{2}{3}$ times more than the small bag. How much does the large bag weigh?

_____ pounds

2. The medium bag of sand weighs $2\frac{1}{4}$ times more than the small bag. The small bag of sand weighs $5\frac{1}{2}$ pounds. How much does the medium bag weigh?

_____ pounds

3. The large bag of sand weighs $3\frac{3}{4}$ times more than the small bag. How much does the large bag of sand weigh?

_____ pounds

4. The small bag of grass seed weighs $2\frac{1}{4}$ pounds. The medium bag weighs $2\frac{2}{5}$ times more. How much does the medium bag weigh?

_____ pounds

5. The large bag of grass seed weighs $4\frac{2}{3}$ times more than the small bag. How much does the large bag weigh?

_____ pounds

Lesson 5.3 Dividing Whole Numbers and Fractions

Read the problem carefully and solve. Show your work under each question.

Kenesha and Leon need to use colored ribbons for a craft project. They plan to cut each color ribbon into equal parts. The blue ribbon is $\frac{2}{3}$ yard long, and the yellow ribbon is $\frac{3}{4}$ yard long. The white ribbon is $\frac{6}{8}$ yard long, and the red ribbon is $\frac{3}{5}$ yard long.

Helpful Hint

To find the reciprocal of a fraction, reverse the numerator and the denominator. For example, the reciprocal of 8, or $\frac{8}{1}$, is $\frac{1}{8}$.

To divide, multiply by the reciprocal of the divisor. Simplify all fractions.

1. What is the reciprocal of the amount of blue ribbon Kenesha and Leon have?

   _____

2. Kenesha cut the blue ribbon into 4 pieces. What is the length of each piece?

   _____ yard

3. Leon decides to cut the yellow ribbon into 6 pieces. What is the length of each piece?

   _____ yard

4. Kenesha cuts the white ribbon next. She cuts it into 4 pieces. How long is each piece?

   _____ yard

5. Leon cuts the red ribbon in half. What is the length of each piece?

   _____ yard

Lesson 5.4 Dividing Fractions by Fractions

Read the problem carefully and solve. Show your work under each question.

Jonah is helping his grandfather cut 4 pieces of wood. His grandfather plans to cut each piece of wood into equal parts. The first piece of wood is $\frac{3}{4}$ meter long. The second piece of wood is $\frac{4}{5}$ meter long. The third piece is $\frac{2}{3}$ meter long, and the fourth piece is $\frac{7}{8}$ meter long.

Helpful Hint

To divide two fractions, multiply the first fraction by the reciprocal of the second fraction.

$$\frac{3}{4} \div \frac{5}{9} = \frac{3}{4} \times \frac{9}{5}$$

Simplify all fractions.

---

1. Jonah's grandfather cuts the first piece of wood into pieces that are $\frac{1}{3}$ meter long each. How many pieces can be cut?

   _____ pieces

2. Jonah wants to cut the second piece of wood into pieces that are $\frac{2}{3}$ meter long each. How many pieces will he have?

   _____ pieces

3. Jonah's grandfather decides to cut the third piece of wood into pieces that are $\frac{1}{2}$ meter long each. How many pieces will he have?

   _____ pieces

4. Jonah and his grandfather plan to cut the fourth piece of wood into pieces that will be $\frac{1}{4}$ meter long each. How many pieces can be cut?

   _____ pieces

5. Before they cut the fourth piece of wood, Jonah's grandfather decides to cut it into pieces that are $\frac{2}{5}$ meter instead. How many pieces will they have now?

   _____ pieces

Lesson 5.5 Dividing Mixed Numbers

Read the problem carefully and solve. Show your work under each question.

Emilio is having guests over for a cookout. He divides food equally into bowls and containers to serve to his guests.

Helpful Hint

To divide mixed numerals:

1. Rename each mixed numeral as an improper fraction.
2. Multiply by the reciprocal of the divisor.
3. Simplify all fractions.

1. Emilio has $6\frac{1}{4}$ ounces of nuts. He plans to divide the nuts into containers that hold $2\frac{1}{2}$ ounces each. How many containers will he fill?

_____ containers

2. Emilio made $3\frac{3}{4}$ pounds of fruit salad. He plans to divide it evenly into containers that hold $1\frac{2}{5}$ pounds each. How many containers will he fill?

_____ containers

3. Before Emilio divides up the fruit salad, he decides he wants to put it into 3 bowls instead. How many pounds of fruit salad will be in each bowl?

_____ pounds

4. Emilio also has $8\frac{1}{2}$ ounces of salsa. If he divides it into containers that hold $4\frac{1}{4}$ ounces each, how many containers can he fill?

_____ containers

5. Emilio's friend brought $3\frac{3}{5}$ pounds of coleslaw. Emilio plans to divide it into bowls that hold $2\frac{1}{4}$ pounds each. How many bowls will he fill?

_____ containers

Check What You Learned

Multiplying and Dividing Fractions

Read the problem carefully and solve. Show your work under each question.

Adita and Amit want to make a garden. They look for supplies around their house. They find $\frac{3}{5}$ yard of ribbon and a piece of wood $\frac{4}{5}$ meter long. Their mother buys them a $4\frac{3}{4}$-pound bag of fertilizer.

1. Adita and Amit dug up the soil in $\frac{2}{3}$ of the garden before lunch. Amit dug $\frac{1}{4}$ of that amount. What part of the garden did Amit dig?

   _____ of the garden

2. Their dad helps them cut the piece of wood into stakes for the tomato plants. He cuts the wood into equal pieces that are $\frac{1}{3}$ meter long each. How many pieces does he cut?

   _____ pieces

3. Adita plans to tie each of the tomato plants to a stake. She cuts the piece of ribbon into 6 equal pieces. What is the length of each piece?

   _____ yard

4. Adita and Amit spend $1\frac{2}{3}$ hours working on the garden every day. How many hours do they spend working on it in 5 days?

   _____ hours

5. Their mother almost bought a larger bag of fertilizer. The larger bag weighs $2\frac{2}{3}$ times more than the bag she bought for their garden. How much does the larger bag weigh?

   _____ pounds

6. Adita also wants to plant some herbs in pots. She uses a $4\frac{1}{2}$-pound bag of potting soil to fill 6 pots. How many pounds of soil will be in each pot if she puts the same amount of soil in each?

   _____ pound

Check What You Know

Adding and Subtracting Decimals

Read the problem carefully and solve. Show your work under each question.

Clara needs to restock some of the art and craft supplies in her store. She checks the shelves to see which items she needs to order.

1. Clara notices that she is low on lace trim and silver ribbon. She has 42.81 centimeters left of lace trim and 42.08 centimeters left of silver ribbon. Compare the two decimals using <, >, or =.

_____

2. Write the decimal 42.08 in words.

_____

_____

3. Clara finds that she has plenty of molds but only one bag of plaster left. It weighs $4\frac{1}{4}$ pounds. What is the weight of the bag written as a decimal?

_____ pounds

4. Clara wants to buy more glitter. The last container weighs 0.24 kilogram. What is the weight of the glitter written as a fraction?

_____ kilogram

5. The bags of colored sand come in two sizes, small and large. Clara decides to order both sizes. The large bag weighs 2.72 kilograms. The small bag weighs 0.54 kilogram. What is the difference in weight of the two bags?

_____ kilograms

6. Clara needs to order some painting supplies. She plans to spend $73.99 on bottles of colored paint, $154.50 on canvas, and $32.98 on brushes. How much altogether will she spend?

_____

Lesson 6.1 Tenths, Hundredths, Thousandths, and Ten Thousandths

Read the problem carefully and solve. Show your work under each question.

Eric uses a special tool to take precise measurements of some small engine parts. The tool can measure up to a ten thousandth of an inch. The first measurement he took was 0.178 inch, and the second measurement was 0.0157 inch. The next measurement was 0.34 inch.

Helpful Hint

Decimal places from greatest to least:

tenths --------→ 0.1
hundredths --------→ 0.01
thousandths --------→ 0.001
ten thousandths --------→ 0.0001

1. What digit is in the hundredths place in the decimal 0.0157?

_____

2. What digit is in the ten thousandths place in the decimal 0.0157?

_____

3. Write the decimal 0.178 in words.

_____

4. Write the decimal 0.34 in words.

_____

5. Eric's final measurement was one and three hundred eight thousandths inches. Write this decimal in standard form.

_____ inches

Lesson 6.2 Changing Fractions to Decimals

Read the problem carefully and solve. Show your work under each question.

Lian, Jason, Melvin, and Ella all collect different sized rocks to study in their science class. They each weigh their favorite rock and record the weight. Lian's rock weighs $\frac{3}{5}$ pound. Jason's rock weighs $\frac{6}{25}$ pound. Melvin's rock weighs $1\frac{3}{4}$ pounds, and Ella's rock weighs $3\frac{4}{5}$ pounds. Their teacher asks them to convert the fractions into decimals.

Helpful Hint

Change $\frac{1}{5}$ to tenths: $\frac{1}{5} = \frac{1 \times 2}{5 \times 2} = \frac{2}{10} = 0.2$

Change $\frac{1}{4}$ to hundredths:

$$\frac{1}{4} = \frac{1 \times 25}{4 \times 25} = \frac{25}{100} = 0.25$$

1. What is the weight of Lian's rock in tenths?

_____ pound

2. Write the weight of Melvin's rock in hundredths.

_____ pounds

3. What is the weight of Jason's rock in thousandths?

_____ pound

4. How much does Ella's rock weigh in hundredths?

_____ pounds

5. Ella decides to find out how much her rock weighs in thousandths instead. What is its weight?

_____ pounds

Lesson 6.3 Changing Decimals to Fractions

Read the problem carefully and solve. Show your work under each question.

Lian, Jason, Melvin, and Ella collect more rocks for their science class. This time, they each weigh their rocks in kilograms. Lian's rock weighs 2.15 kilograms. Jason's rock weighs 0.225 kilogram. Melvin's rock weighs 1.07 kilograms, and Ella's rock weighs 0.42 kilogram. Their teacher asks them to convert the decimals into fractions or mixed numerals.

Helpful Hint

Change 0.12 into a fraction:

$$0.12 = \frac{12}{100} = \frac{3}{25}$$

Remember to simplify all fractions.

1. What is the weight of Lian's rock written as a fraction or mixed numeral?

   _____ kilograms

2. Write the weight of Melvin's rock as a fraction or mixed numeral.

   _____ kilograms

3. What is the weight of Ella's rock written as a fraction or mixed numeral?

   _____ kilogram

4. Write the weight of Jason's rock as a fraction or mixed numeral.

   _____ kilogram

5. Jason found another rock. It weighed 1.28 kilograms. What is the weight of this rock written as a fraction or mixed numeral?

   _____ kilograms

Lesson 6.4 Comparing and Ordering Decimals

Read the problem carefully and solve. Show your work under each question.

Theresa's class grows plants for a science experiment. Each student plants a few seeds in a pot. Once the seeds sprout, the students record their plants' heights each day.

Helpful Hint

To order a group of decimals:

1. Line up the decimal points of all the numbers.
2. Compare the digits in each place from left to right.
3. List the decimals in order from least to greatest.

1. Theresa and Keri compare the height of their plants. Theresa's plant is 3.12 centimeters tall, and Keri's plant is 3.02 centimeters tall. Compare the two heights using <, >, or =.

_____

2. Ramon's plant is 4.92 centimeters tall, and Trisha's plant is 5.3 centimeters tall. Compare the two heights using <, >, or =.

_____

3. After a few weeks, Keri and Ramon compare the height of their plants. Keri's plant is 8.12 centimeters tall, and Ramon's plant is 8.13 centimeters tall. Compare the two heights using <, >, or =.

_____

4. Four students in the class want to organize their plants by height. The heights of their plants in centimeters are: 6.01, 5.06, 4.96, 5.61. Order these decimals from least to greatest.

_____

_____

5. One day, Theresa and Trisha convert their plant's heights from centimeters to meters. They calculate that Theresa's plant is 0.073 meter tall, and Trisha's is 0.070 meter tall. Compare the two heights using <, >, or =.

_____

Lesson 6.5 Adding and Subtracting Money

Read the problem carefully and solve. Show your work under each question.

Jamie and Roberto are grand prize winners of a contest. They each win a $200 shopping spree at their favorite stores. Both can spend under that amount but cannot spend more.

> **Helpful Hint**
>
> Always line up the decimal points before adding or subtracting money. Be sure to include the decimal point and dollar sign in your answer.

1. Jamie buys three items that cost $9.47, $19.68, and $67.94. What is the total amount of money she spends on these three items?

_____

2. Roberto is deciding between two pairs of basketball sneakers. One pair costs $64.95, and the other costs $75.99. What is the difference between the two prices?

_____

3. Roberto buys the sneakers for $64.95. How much money does he have left to spend?

_____

4. The next item Jamie wants to buy costs $112.98. Does she have enough money left to buy it? If not, by how much will she be over?

_____

_____

5. The company who sponsored the contest spent $3,256.57 altogether on promoting and advertising the contest. What is the difference between this amount and the amount Jamie and Roberto won altogether?

_____

Check What You Learned

Adding and Subtracting Decimals

Read the problem carefully and solve. Show your work under each question.

Mr. Perez's class sets up a tropical fish tank. They need to collect all the supplies before they can put it together. Many of the students volunteer to bring in items from home.

1. Charlie brings in a few plants to put into the aquarium. He measures the height of the two tallest ones. One of the plants is 16.57 centimeters tall, and the other is 16.75 centimeters tall. Compare the two decimals using $<$, $>$, or $=$.

   _____

2. Write the decimal 16.57 in words.

   _____

   _____

3. Yori brings in a bag of tank gravel. It weighs $2\frac{1}{5}$ pounds. What is the weight of the gravel written as a decimal?

   _____ pounds

4. Angela brings in some fish food. The label on the container says it contains 0.68 kilogram of fish food. What is the weight of the fish food written as a fraction?

   _____ kilogram

5. Marco brings in two rocks to put into the aquarium. He weighs each rock. One weighs 1.814 kilograms, and the other weighs 0.92 kilogram. What is the difference in weight between the two rocks?

   _____ kilogram

6. Mr. Perez bought a fish filter for $28.99, a heater for $16.79, and a small net for $3.98. How much altogether did he spend?

   _____

Mid-Test Chapters 1–6

Read the problem carefully and solve. Show your work under each question.

Diane compares her two favorite football players. Randy played quarterback for 14 years, throwing for a total of 36,218 yards, with 265 touchdowns and 143 interceptions. Trevor played quarterback for 16 years, throwing for a total of 46,728 yards, with 288 touchdowns and 238 interceptions.

1. How many more touchdowns than interceptions did Randy have?

_____

2. How many interceptions altogether did both players have?

_____ interceptions

3. How many total yards did both players throw?

_____ yards

4. Randy played a total of 210 games. Each year, he played in the same number of games. How many games did he play in each year?

_____ games

5. Trevor played in 13 games every season. How many games altogether did he play?

_____ games

6. During Randy's first 6 years playing quarterback, he scored 134 touchdowns. He scored about the same number of touchdowns each of those years. Estimate to find about how many touchdowns he scored each year in his first 6 years.

about _____ touchdowns

Mid-Test Chapters 1–6

Read the problem carefully and solve. Show your work under each question.

Kelly plans to paint the walls inside the community center in her town. She buys cans of paint in yellow, green, blue, red, and white. She plans to paint the walls on the first floor and then the walls on the second floor.

---

1. Kelly will paint 20 walls on the first floor of the community center and 28 walls on the second floor. What is the greatest common factor of these numbers?

_____

2. Kelly will paint $\frac{1}{4}$ of the walls on the first floor and $\frac{3}{7}$ of the walls on the second floor green. Rename these two fractions with common denominators.

_____ and _____

3. Kelly uses $\frac{14}{6}$ cans of yellow paint for the walls on the first floor. Write this improper fraction as a mixed numeral in its simplest form.

_____

4. After painting the first floor, Kelly has used part of 2 cans of blue paint. She has used $\frac{6}{7}$ of one can and $\frac{3}{7}$ of the other can. How many cans of blue paint did Kelly use in all?

_____ cans

5. After painting the first floor, Kelly has used part of 2 cans of white paint. She has used $\frac{3}{5}$ of one can and $\frac{5}{6}$ of the other can. How many cans of white paint did Kelly use in all?

_____ cans

6. Kelly uses a total of $5\frac{2}{9}$ cans of white paint and $\frac{6}{7}$ can of red paint. How many total cans of paint does Kelly use?

_____ cans

Mid-Test Chapters 1–6

Read the problem carefully and solve. Show your work under each question.

Juan makes fruit smoothies for his friends and family at a party. In each smoothie, Juan blends $\frac{5}{6}$ cup of low fat yogurt, $\frac{1}{2}$ cup of milk, $1\frac{1}{5}$ cups of raspberries, $\frac{3}{4}$ cups of strawberries, and $1\frac{2}{3}$ cups of ice.

1. Juan's little sister Camila wants a smoothie that is only $\frac{1}{2}$ the size of a normal smoothie. How many cups of yogurt should Juan use to make Camila's smoothie?

_____ cup

2. Juan's friends, Brian and Sharon, each want a smoothie. How many total cups of strawberries will Juan use to make both smoothies?

_____ cups

3. Juan makes a large smoothie for his parents to share. He makes the smoothie $2\frac{1}{4}$ times the size of his recipe. How many cups of raspberries does he use?

_____ cups

4. Juan starts with 15 cups of milk. How many smoothies can he make with this amount of milk?

_____ smoothies

5. Juan's little cousin Miguel wants a small smoothie, so Juan uses $\frac{5}{18}$ cup of yogurt. What is the reciprocal of $\frac{5}{18}$ written in its simplest form?

_____

6. Juan starts with $15\frac{1}{9}$ cups of ice. How many smoothies can he make with this amount of ice?

_____ smoothies

Mid-Test Chapters 1–6

Read the problem carefully and solve. Show your work under each question.

Last week, the weather station announced that the rainfall was 0.24 inch for Monday, 0.76 inch for Tuesday, and 1.63 inches for Wednesday.

---

1. Write the decimal for Wednesday's rainfall in words.

_____

2. Write the decimal for Monday's rainfall as a fraction or mixed numeral in its simplest form.

_____ inch

3. The local newspaper predicted that there would be $2\frac{3}{10}$ inches of rain this weekend. Write this mixed number as a decimal.

_____ inches

4. Compare the rainfall on Tuesday and Wednesday by using <, >, or =.

0.76 inch _____ 1.63 inches

5. What is the difference in the amount of rain that fell on Monday and the amount of rain that fell on Wednesday?

_____ inches

6. A worker at the weather station wants to buy 2 new measuring instruments for the station. She buys a thermometer for $2.32 and a barometer for $5.84. How much altogether does she spend?

_____

NAME _____

 Check What You Know

Multiplying and Dividing Decimals

Read the problem carefully and solve. Show your work under each question.

Roger lives 4.3 miles from where he works. Five days a week, Roger either walks the 4.3 miles or takes a bus to work. The bus takes a route that goes 5.7 miles before arriving near his workplace. The bus costs $1.35 each trip. Roger always gets a ride home from his coworker, David.

1. If Roger walks to work 5 times, how many miles does he walk?

_____ miles

2. One month during the winter, Roger took the bus 21 times in the morning. How much did he pay in bus fare for the month?

_____

3. Another month, Roger walked to work 19 times. How many miles did he walk in all?

_____ miles

4. During one week, Roger rode the bus for 17.1 miles. How many days did Roger ride the bus that week?

_____ days

5. David uses 0.3 gallon of gasoline to drive Roger home every day. If David uses 6.3 gallons driving Roger during one month, how many times does he drive Roger home?

_____ times

6. The cost of bus fare rose to $1.62 per trip. Roger spent $19.44 on the bus that month. How many trips did he take?

_____ trips

Lesson 7.1 Multiplying Decimals and Money

Read the problem carefully and solve. Show your work under each question.

Pedro buys food at the grocery store. His grocery list includes bananas, grapes, cereal, and soup.

1. Pedro buys 4 bananas. The bananas he picks out each weigh 3.95 ounces. What is the total weight of all 4 bananas?

_____ ounces

Helpful Hint

There are no U.S. coins worth less than $0.01, so when finding the cost of an item, round your answer to the nearest hundredth of a dollar.

4. Pedro buys grapes for $0.88 cents per pound. When the cashier weighs the grapes, the weight is 6.72 pounds. What is the total cost of the grapes?

_____

2. There are two different boxes of Pedro's favorite cereal at the grocery store. The larger box weighs 14.5 ounces. The smaller box weighs 0.65 times the larger box. How much does the smaller box weigh?

_____ ounces

5. The total cost of the food Pedro buys is $87.35. If Pedro spends the same amount on groceries every week, how much will he spend in 13 weeks?

_____

3. A can of soup costs $1.29. If Pedro buys 8 cans of soup, how much does he spend?

_____

Lesson 7.2 Dividing by Decimals

Read the problem carefully and solve. Show your work under each question.

Calvin owns an office supply store. He orders boxes of new supplies for his store every week. The place where he orders from ships boxes based on their weight in kilograms. Calvin wants to know how many supplies come in each box.

Helpful Hint

Multiply the divisor and dividend by 10, 100, or 1,000 to change the divisor to a whole number.

Example:

$$0.8\overline{)72.0} \dashrightarrow 8\overline{)720}$$

Multiply by 10

1. Calvin orders scissors. Each pair of scissors weighs 0.4 kilogram. A box of scissors weighs 35.2 kilograms. How many pairs of scissors come in each box?

_____ pairs of scissors

2. Scented markers each weigh 0.02 kilogram. A box of these markers weighs 8 kilograms. How many markers come in a box?

_____ markers

3. The staplers that Calvin orders each weigh 0.7 kilogram. One box of staplers weighs 4.9 kilograms. How many staplers come in one box?

_____ staplers

4. The paper clips Calvin orders for his store weigh 0.002 kilogram each. Each box has 4.5 kilograms of paper clips. How many paper clips are in each box?

_____ paper clips

5. Calvin ordered several boxes of pens. Each pen weighs 0.009 kilogram. Each box weighs 36 kilograms. How many pens are in each box?

_____ pens

Lesson 7.3 Dividing Money

Read the problem carefully and solve. Show your work under each question.

The department store in Lisa's town is having a special sale on a few items. The total sales during one day for the discounted items are on the chart to the right.

Items	Total Sales
Cameras	$365.61
Towels	$56.80
DVDs	$270.00
Microwaves	$227.50
Books	$405.00

Helpful Hint

When working with decimals in money, be sure to show your answer to the hundredths place.

No: $2.4   Yes: $2.40

Add zero to show 40 cents

1. The department store sold 8 of the sale towels. How much did each towel cost?

   _____

2. The department store sold DVDs for $18.00 each. How many did they sell?

   _____ DVDs

3. The store sold 5 of the sale microwaves. What was the sale price for each microwave?

   _____

4. The books were on sale for $9.00 each. How many books did the store sell?

   _____ books

5. The store sold 7 cameras. How much did each camera cost?

   _____

Check What You Learned

Multiplying and Dividing Decimals

Read the problem carefully and solve. Show your work under each question.

The general store in Katie's town sells 5 different types of nuts by the pound: almonds, cashews, peanuts, pecans, and pistachios.

1. The peanuts cost $2.70 for 1 pound. How much does 3.5 pounds of peanuts cost?

_____

2. The general store has 2 different sized bags. The small bag holds 2.83 pounds of peanuts. The large bag is 2.2 times the size of the small bag. How many pounds of peanuts can the large bag hold?

_____ pounds

3. Katie buys 3.43 pounds of cashews for a party. She wants to divide the cashews evenly into 7 bowls. How many pounds of peanuts will she put in each bowl?

_____ pound

4. Katie also buys 16.5 pounds of pecans for baking pies. If she uses 0.5 pound of pecans for each pie, how many pies can she make?

_____ pies

5. Almonds cost $4.00 per pound. A cook from the local bakery buys $96.00 worth of almonds. How many pounds does he buy?

_____ pounds

6. A bag of pistachios that weighs 6 pounds costs $50.70. How much do the pistachios cost per pound?

_____ per pound

Check What You Know

Finding Percents

Read the problem carefully and solve. Show your work under each question.

Chet buys party supplies. He buys bags of confetti and bags of balloons. He also buys two banners: one $6\frac{1}{4}$ feet long and one 10.5 feet long.

---

1. Chet buys a bag of balloons. He finds that 14% of the balloons in the bag are red. What is this percent written as a decimal?

_____

2. A bag of confetti weighs $\frac{3}{5}$ pound. What is $\frac{3}{5}$ written as a percent?

_____

3. Chet buys a bag of confetti and will use 65% of this confetti at the next school dance. How is 65% written as a decimal?

_____

4. Chet buys a bag of 32 balloons. He blows up 75% of the balloons. How many balloons does he blow up?

_____ balloons

5. Chet writes "Happy Birthday" across 20% of the small banner. What is the length of this message?

_____ feet

6. Chet writes "Congratulations" across 62% of the large banner. How long is this message?

_____ feet

Lesson 8.1 Percent to Fraction and Fraction to Percent

Read the problem carefully and solve. Show your work under each question.

On Monday, all of the students at Central Elementary School took a survey about their favorite classes and activities.

Helpful Hint

Percent to fraction:

$$40\% = 40 \times \frac{1}{100} = \frac{40}{100} = \frac{2}{5}$$

Fraction to percent:

$$\frac{1}{4} \times \frac{25}{25} = \frac{25}{100} = 25\%$$

1. The survey found that 30% of the students chose math as their favorite subject. Write this percent as a fraction in simplest form.

_____

2. The survey found that $\frac{13}{25}$ of the students play sports after school. Write this fraction as a percent.

_____

3. Forty-five percent of the students walk to school. What fraction of the students walk to school?

_____

4. The survey found that 38% of the students at Central Elementary chose social studies as their favorite subject. Write this percent as a fraction.

_____

5. The survey found that $\frac{13}{20}$ of the students bring their lunch to school each day. What is this fraction written as a percent?

_____

Lesson 8.2 Percent to Decimal and Decimal to Percent

Read the problem carefully and solve. Show your work under each question.

Juanita has a vegetable garden in her backyard. In her garden, she grows cabbage, cucumbers, carrots, peppers, and zucchini.

Helpful Hint

Percent to decimal:

$$25\% = 25 \times 0.01 = 0.25$$

Decimal to percent:

$$0.73 \times \frac{0.73}{1} = \frac{0.73 \times 100}{100} = 73\%$$

1. 32% of the vegetables in Juanita's garden are carrots. How is this percent written as a decimal?

_____

2. Juanita finds that 0.13 of her garden is pepper plants. What is this decimal written as a percent?

_____

3. Juanita checks her zucchinis. She finds that bugs have eaten 4.5% of her zucchini crop. What is this percent as a decimal?

_____

4. Juanita decides to pick the cucumbers. After an hour, she has picked 78% of the cucumbers. What is this percent written as a decimal?

_____

5. Juanita finds that 0.27 of her garden is cabbage. What is this decimal written as a percent?

_____

Lesson 8.3 Multiplying by Fractions

Read the problem carefully and solve. Show your work under each question.

Marcia made trail mix for her friends and family. The trail mix has raisins, cashews, sunflower seeds, pretzels, and almonds. She made a total of 78 ounces of trail mix. So far, she has given 7 ounces of trail mix to her friend Dana, 20 ounces of trail mix to her brother, and 15 ounces of trail mix to her parents.

Helpful Hint

20% of $10 = 20\% \times 10$

$\quad = \frac{20}{100} \times \frac{10}{1}$

$\quad = \frac{1}{100}$

$\quad = 2$

1. Dana ate her trail mix. She found that 28% of the trail mix is raisins. What is 28% of 7 ounces?

_____ ounces

2. Marcia's brother ate his trail mix. He found that 6% of the trail mix is sunflower seeds. What is 6% of 20 ounces?

_____ ounces

3. Marcia's parents ate their trail mix. 17% of the trail mix is cashews. What is 17% of 15 ounces?

_____ ounces

4. When Marcia made the trail mix, she made it with 25% almonds. How many ounces of almonds did she use?

_____ ounces

5. When Marcia made the trail mix, she made it with 24% pretzels. How many ounces of pretzels did she use?

_____ ounces

Lesson 8.4 Multiplying by Decimals

Read the problem carefully and solve. Show your work under each question.

Mr. Foster drives a school bus. Every time students at Central Elementary School take a field trip, Mr. Foster drives them there. Mr. Foster makes a stop along each trip so that the students can eat lunch.

Helpful Hint

20% of 15.2 = 0.2 × 15.2

= 7.1

---

1. One day, a class takes a trip to an apple orchard 29 miles away. Mr. Foster stops for a lunch break 11% of the way to the orchard. How far did Mr. Foster drive before stopping?

_____ miles

2. Another day, a class takes a trip to the science museum 40 miles away. Mr. Foster stops for a lunch break 26% of the way there. How far did Mr. Foster drive before stopping?

_____ miles

3. Mr. Foster drives a group of students to the beach 45 miles from the school. He stops the bus for a break after driving 20% of the total distance. How far did Mr. Foster drive before stopping?

_____ miles

4. Mr. Foster drives a group of students to the art museum 95 miles from the school. After driving 40% of the way there, Mr. Foster stops for lunch. How far did Mr. Foster drive before stopping?

_____ miles

5. A group of students tour a factory 80 miles from the school. Mr. Foster buys gasoline for the bus 80% of the way there. How far did he drive before buying gas?

_____ miles

Lesson 8.5 Ratios

Read the problem carefully and solve. Show your work under each question.

A ratio is the comparison of two quantities or measures. A comparison of 6 apples and 9 bananas can be expressed as $\frac{6}{9}$, 6 to 9, or 6:9. If the number of apples is represented by black circles, and the number of bananas is represented by white circles, this ratio could be modeled as:

Marc is at the grocery store. Help him solve the following problems.

---

1. There are 16 grapes for every 3 peaches in a fruit cup. What is the ratio of the number of grapes to the number of peaches?

_____

2. The price of 5 pounds of carrots is $10. How many dollars per pound are carrots?

_____

3. There are 4 containers of peanut butter for every 18 crackers. What is the ratio of the number of peanut butter containers to the number of crackers?

_____

4. Marc can jar 16 liters of jam after 4 days. How much jam will he jar if he spends 5 days making jam?

_____ liters

5. There are 8 men in the grocery store coffee shop for every 6 women. What is the ratio of the number of men to the number of women?

_____

Lesson 8.6 Ratios and Rates

Read the problem carefully and solve. Show your work under each question.

Ratios and rates can be used in ratio tables and graphs to solve problems.

A bookstore is having a sale. All paperback books are $6 each.
Two books cost $12 and 3 books cost $18.

$$2 \times \$6 = \$12$$
$$3 \times \$6 = \$18$$

---

1. Fill in the table for the cost of 4 books, 5 books, and 6 books. Multiply to find the answers.

Number of Books (n)	Cost (c)
1	$6
2	$12
3	$18
4	
5	
6	
7	
8	
9	

3. Plot the ratios for the cost of 1 book, 2 books, 3 books, and 4 books on the graph.

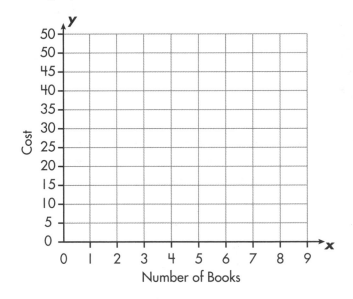

2. Fill in the table for the cost of 7 books, 8 books, and 9 books.

4. Plot the ratios for the cost of 5 books, 6 books, 7 books, 8 books, and 9 books on the graph.

Check What You Learned

Finding Percents

Read the problem carefully and solve. Show your work under each question.

Ms. O'Conner's class is staying after school to decorate the classroom for school spirit week. Ms. O'Conner brought pizza and fruit juice for the class.

1. Twenty-two percent of the juice that Ms. O'Conner brought is apple juice. How is 22% written as a decimal?

_____

2. Ms. O'Conner says that 0.6 of one pizza has mushrooms on top. How is 0.6 written as a percent?

_____

3. After an hour, 84% of a bottle of orange juice is gone. How is 84% written as a decimal?

_____

4. Ms. O'Conner has 25 students in her class. Ten are boys and 15 are girls. What is the ratio of the number of boys to the number of girls?

_____

5. Ms. O'Conner brought 5 pizzas. The students eat 78% of the pizza. How many pizzas do they eat? Write your answer as a fraction.

_____ pizzas

6. In total, Ms. O'Conner brought 8 gallons of juice. The students drink 42% of the juice. How many gallons of juice do they drink? Write your answer as a decimal.

_____ gallons

Check What You Know

Customary Measurement

Read the problem carefully and solve. Show your work under each question.

Kristen invited her friends over for lunch. She is serving sandwiches and fruit juice on a table in the dining room.

---

1. Kristen uses 48 ounces of ingredients to make her sandwiches. How many pounds of ingredients does she use?

_____ lb.

2. After Kristen makes each sandwich, she cuts it in half to make triangles. One half of a sandwich is shown below. What is the area of the triangle?

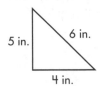

5 in.   6 in.

4 in.

_____ sq. in.

3. What is the perimeter of the triangle above?

_____ in.

4. Kristen has 16 pints of fruit juice. How many gallons of fruit juice does she have?

_____ gal.

5. Kristen places the sandwiches on the dining room table. The table is 8 feet long. How many inches long is the table?

_____ in.

6. Kristen puts a rectangular vase in the middle of the table. What is the volume of the vase?

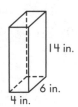

14 in.

6 in.

4 in.

_____ cu. in.

Lesson 9.1 Units of Length (inches, feet, yards, and miles)

Read the problem carefully and solve. Show your work under each question.

Dara is doing chores and running errands today. She wants to clean her kitchen, rake leaves, buy a plant, and shop for groceries.

Helpful Hint

1 foot (ft.) = 12 inches (in.)
1 yard (yd.) = 3 ft.
1 yd. = 36 in.
1 mile (mi.) = 5,280 ft.
1 mi. = 1,760 yd.

1. Dara cleans her kitchen first. She washes her kitchen counter, which is 7 feet long. How many inches long is the counter?

_____ in.

2. Next, Dara rakes leaves along the side of the driveway. The driveway is 81 feet long. How many yards long is Dara's driveway?

_____ yd.

3. Dara drives to a greenhouse to buy flowers for her garden. The greenhouse is 2,640 feet from Dara's house. How many miles from Dara's house is the greenhouse?

_____ mi.

4. At the greenhouse, Dara buys a fern that is 3 feet and 4 inches tall. How many inches tall is this plant?

_____ in.

5. On her way home, Dara buys groceries from the supermarket. The supermarket is 3 miles from her house. How many yards are equal to 3 miles?

_____ yd.

Lesson 9.2 Liquid Volume (cups, pints, quarts, and gallons)

Read the problem carefully and solve. Show your work under each question.

Jacob tries to conserve water by keeping track of how much water he uses. He keeps track of the total amount of water he uses around his house during one day.

Helpful Hint

1 pint (pt.) = 2 cups (c.)
1 quart (qt.) = 2 pt.
1 gallon (gal.) = 4 qt.

1. Jacob uses 2 quarts of water to cook pasta. How many pints of water does he use?

_____ pt.

2. Jacob needs to water his plants, so he fills up a 1-gallon jug with water. How many pints of water does he use?

_____ pt.

3. To take a bath, Jacob uses 25 gallons of water. How many quarts of water does Jacob use?

_____ qt.

4. During the day, Jacob drinks a total of 8 cups of water. How many gallons of water are equal to 8 cups?

_____ gal.

5. Jacob uses 8 gallons of water to wash dishes. How many cups of water does he use?

_____ c.

Lesson 9.3 Weight (ounces, pounds, and tons)

Read the problem carefully and solve. Show your work under each question.

Diego packs his car for a camping trip. At the campsite, he and his friends will have to park the car and then walk to the campsite. Diego wants to weigh all of the items that he packs in the car to keep track of how much they will have to carry to the campsite.

Helpful Hint

1 pound (lb.) = 16 ounces (oz.)
1 ton (T.) = 2,000 lb.
1 T. = 32,000 oz.

1. Diego packs a backpack of supplies. The backpack weighs 128 ounces. How many pounds does the backpack weigh?

    _____ lb.

2. Diego wants to bring his bicycle, which weighs 22 pounds. How many ounces does his bicycle weigh?

    _____ oz.

3. Diego and his friends tie a canoe to the roof of the car. The canoe weighs 60 pounds. How many ounces does the canoe weigh?

    _____ oz.

4. After packing the car, Diego's car weighs a total of 3,000 pounds. How many tons does Diego's car weigh?

    _____ T.

5. Diego's friend, Marcia, also packs her van. After packing, Marcia's van weighs 2.5 tons. How many pounds does Marcia's van weigh?

    _____ lb.

Lesson 9.4 Measuring Perimeter, Area, and Volume

Read the problem carefully and solve. Show your work under each question.

Mr. Adams had his students cut shapes out of construction paper for a game he wants to play with his class. In this game, students choose shapes out of a box. He had his students cut out triangles and 4-sided shapes.

Helpful Hint

Triangle area formula:

$$A = \frac{1}{2} \times b \times h$$

Rectangular solid volume formula:

$$V = l \times w \times h$$

1. Ron cut out the rectangle below. What is the perimeter of the rectangle?

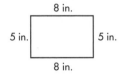

_____ in.

2. Melissa cut out the trapezoid below. What is the perimeter of the trapezoid?

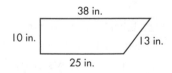

_____ in.

3. Carlos cut out the right triangle below. What is the area of the triangle?

_____ sq. in.

4. Jackie cut out the right triangle below. What is the area of the triangle?

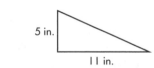

_____ sq. in.

5. Mr. Adams put the shapes in the box shown below. What is the volume of the box?

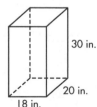

_____ cu. in.

Check What You Learned

Customary Measurement

Read the problem carefully and solve. Show your work under each question.

Mr. Clark wants a pool so that he can swim laps each morning before he leaves for work. He decides to have a lap pool built in his backyard.

---

1. The right triangle below shows the shape of Mr. Clark's backyard. What is the perimeter of his backyard?

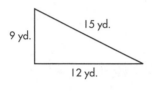

9 yd.   15 yd.   12 yd.

_____ yd.

2. What is the length of the longest side of the triangle above in feet?

_____ ft.

3. What is the area of Mr. Clark's backyard?

_____ sq. yd.

4. The blueprint measurements of Mr. Clark's pool are shown below. What is the volume of the pool?

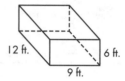

12 ft.   6 ft.   9 ft.

_____ cu. ft.

5. Mr. Clark needs 9 tons of concrete to build the pool. How many pounds are in 9 tons?

_____ lb.

6. Before Mr. Clark can fill his pool with water, he has to paint the inside with a special coating. He buys 5 gallons of this coating. How many quarts of the coating does he buy?

_____ qt.

Check What You Know

Metric Measurement

Read the problem carefully and solve. Show your work under each question.

The Berry Juice Company is introducing a new drink, Blueberry Punch. Samantha is in charge of designing the packaging for the new drink, including the bottle and the label on the bottle.

1. Samantha wants to package the drink in a bottle that is 20 centimeters tall. How many millimeters tall is the bottle?

_____ mm

2. The bottle will have a liquid volume capacity of 0.5 liters. What is the liquid volume capacity of the bottle in milliliters?

_____ mL

3. Each bottle, when filled with Blueberry Punch, will weigh 500 grams. How many kilograms will each bottle weigh?

_____ kg

4. The bottle's label will have the same dimensions as the rectangle below. What is the perimeter of the label?

4 cm
20 cm
20 cm
4 cm

_____ cm

5. What is the area of the label?

_____ sq. cm

6. The factory will pack the bottles of Blueberry Punch in boxes. Each box will weigh 28 pounds when filled. To convert pounds to kilograms, multiply by 0.454. Rounding to the nearest hundredth, what will each box weigh in kilograms?

_____ kg

Lesson 10.1 Units of Length (millimeters, centimeters, meters, and kilometers)

Read the problem carefully and solve. Show your work under each question.

Callie took a trip to France last summer. She writes a paper about the famous buildings in Paris for her social studies class.

Helpful Hint

Millimeters (mm), **centimeters** (cm), **meters** (m), and **kilometers** (km) are metric measures of length.

10 mm = 1 cm	1 mm = 0.1 cm
1,000 mm = 1 m	1 mm = 0.001 m
100 cm = 1 m	1 cm = 0.01 m
1,000 m = 1 km	1 m = 0.001 km

1. Before she writes her paper, Callie checks out books from the library. The library is 2 kilometers from her house. How many meters are equal to 2 kilometers?

_____ m

2. One of Callie's library books is 6 centimeters thick. How many millimeters thick is the book?

_____ mm

3. Callie writes her report on paper that is 250 millimeters wide. How many meters wide is the paper?

_____ m

4. In her report, Callie writes that the Eiffel Tower is 324 meters tall. How many kilometers tall is the Eiffel Tower?

_____ km

5. Callie also writes that the Arc de Triomphe, another Paris landmark, is 49.5 meters tall. How many centimeters are equal to 49.5 meters?

_____ cm

Lesson 10.2 Liquid Volume (milliliters, liters, and kiloliters)

Read the problem carefully and solve. Show your work under each question.

Last week, the supermarket sold 5,253 liters of water. The supermarket sells water in bottles of 10 liters, 4 liters, 1 liter, and 250 milliliters.

Helpful Hint

Milliliters (mL), **liters** (L), and **kiloliters** (kL), are metric measures of liquid volume.

$1 L = 1,000 mL$
$1 kL = 1,000 L$
$1 mL = 0.001 L$
$1 L = 0.001 kL$

---

1. Mr. Chan buys a 4-liter bottle of water. How many milliliters of water does he buy?

   _____ mL

2. Ms. Thompson buys 2 of the 250-milliliter bottles. How many liters of water altogether does she buy?

   _____ L

3. Ms. Santos buys 1 of the 10-liter bottles and 2 of the 1-liter bottles. How many kiloliters of water does she buy in all?

   _____ kL

4. How many kiloliters of water did the supermarket sell last week?

   _____ kL

5. One day last week, the supermarket sold 0.98 kiloliter of water. How many liters did they sell that day?

   _____ L

Lesson 10.3 Weight (milligrams, grams, and kilograms)

Read the problem carefully and solve. Show your work under each question.

Anna buys school supplies. She buys 2 packs of pencils, 10 pens, 3 notebooks, a stapler, and an electric pencil sharpener. She wants to know the weight of each item.

Helpful Hint

Milligrams (mg), **grams** (g), and **kilograms** (kg), are metric measures of weight.

1 g = 1,000 mg	1 mg = 0.001 g
1 kg = 1,000 g	1 g = 0.001 kg

1. The stapler weighs 680 grams. How many kilograms does the stapler weigh?

   _____ kg

2. The 3 notebooks have a combined weight of 1.6 kilograms. How many grams do the notebooks weigh?

   _____ g

3. The electric pencil sharpener weighs 1,800 grams. How many kilograms does it weigh?

   _____ kg

4. Each pen weighs 59 grams. What is the combined weight in milligrams of the 10 pens Anna buys?

   _____ mg

5. One pack of pencils weighs 135,000 milligrams. What is the combined weight, in grams, of the packs of pencils Anna buys?

   _____ g

Lesson 10.4 Measuring Perimeter, Area, and Volume

Read the problem carefully and solve. Show your work under each question.

Don builds a jewelry box for his mother. He wants the jewelry box to have a length of 20 centimeters, a width of 8 centimeters, and a height of 8 centimeters. To build this, Don will need 6 pieces of wood: 2 pieces shaped like squares, and 4 pieces shaped like rectangles.

Helpful Hint

The **perimeter** of a shape is the sum of the lengths of the sides.

The **area** of a rectangle is found by multiplying the length by the width.

The **volume** of a rectangular solid is found by multiplying the length, width, and height.

1. The 2 square-shaped pieces of wood Don uses are the same size. One of the squares is shown below. What is the perimeter of the square?

8 cm

8 cm

_____ cm

2. What is the area of each square-shaped piece of wood that Don uses?

_____ sq. cm

3. The 4 rectangular-shaped pieces of wood Don uses are the same size. One of the rectangles is shown below. What is the perimeter of the rectangle?

8 cm

20 cm

_____ cm

4. What is the area of each rectangular-shaped piece of wood that Don uses?

_____ sq. cm

5. The rectangular solid below shows the dimensions of the jewelry box when it is completed. What is the volume of the box?

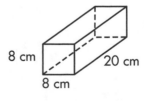

8 cm   20 cm

8 cm

_____ cu. cm

Lesson 10.5 Equivalent Measurements

Read the problem carefully and solve. Show your work under each question.

For a science project, Rachel measured objects in her kitchen. She used the customary system of measurement. Rachel forgot that she was supposed to use the metric system, so she converts each measurement from units in the customary system to units in the metric system.

Helpful Hint

Round each answer to the nearest hundredth.

Example: 3 quarts = _____ liters
$3 \times 0.0946 = 2.838$
3 quarts = 2.84 liters

1. Rachel measured a carton of milk that is 10 inches tall. To convert inches to centimeters, multiply by 2.54. How many centimeters tall is the carton?

_____ cm

2. The carton of milk has a volume of 2 quarts. To convert quarts to liters, multiply by 0.946. How many liters of milk are in the carton?

_____ L

3. Rachel found that a can of soup weighs 11 ounces. To convert ounces to grams, multiply by 28.35. What is the weight of the can in grams?

_____ g

4. The small bottle of orange juice contains 8 liquid ounces. To convert liquid ounces to milliliters, multiply by 29.574. How many milliliters of orange juice are in the bottle?

_____ mL

5. Rachel measures the height of her refrigerator, which is 5 feet tall. To convert feet to meters, multiply by 0.305. How many meters tall is Rachel's refrigerator?

_____ m

Check What You Learned

Customary Measurement

Read the problem carefully and solve. Show your work under each question.

Frank is the architect in charge of the construction of a new two-story building downtown.
He draws the plans and figures out what materials the builders will need.

1. Frank's building will be 8 meters tall. What will the height be in centimeters?

_____ cm

2. Frank thinks the construction workers will have to buy 120 liters of paint for the outside of the building. How many kiloliters of paint will they need?

_____ kL

3. The shape below shows the dimensions of the piece of land that Frank's building will be on. What is the perimeter of the shape?

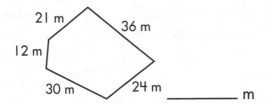

_____ m

4. Frank wants to build a brick walkway to the front door of the building. Each brick weighs 2.7 kilograms. How many grams does each brick weigh?

_____ g

5. Frank draws a rectangular solid to show the dimensions of a room on the first floor. What is the volume of the rectangular solid?

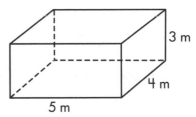

_____ cu. m

6. Frank measures the walkway in front of the house as 6 feet long. To convert feet to meters, multiply by 0.305. What is the length of the walkway in meters?

_____ m

CHAPTER 10 POSTTEST

NAME _____

Check What You Know

Probability and Statistics

Read the problem carefully and solve. Show your work under each question.

The students in Mr. Moore and Ms. Beecher's classes sell raffle tickets to raise money for the school's art program. The line graph on the right shows how many tickets the students in each classroom sold over a 6-week period.

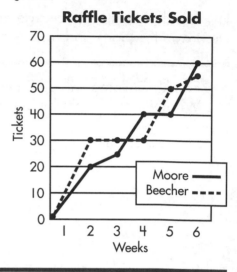

Raffle Tickets Sold

1. After two weeks, how many more tickets did Ms. Beecher's class sell than Mr. Moore's class?

   _____ tickets

2. Which teacher's class sold the most tickets in 6 weeks?

   _____

3. Kevin is in Mr. Moore's class. The number of tickets he sold each week is 4, 3, 1, 4, 0, and 7. What is the mode of this data?

   _____

4. Mr. Moore's class sold the following number of tickets each week for the first 5 weeks: 8, 12, 5, 15, and 0. What is the lower quartile of this data?

   _____

5. Using the number line below, draw a box-and-whisker plot showing the data set for Mr. Moore's class.

   2   4   6   8   10   12   14   16   18   20

6. The students sold a total of 115 tickets. The school principal, Ms. Copeland, bought 25 of these tickets. What is the probability that Ms. Copeland will have the winning raffle ticket?

   _____

Check What You Know

Probability and Statistics

Read the problem carefully and solve. Show your work under each question.

Janet wants to play a sport this winter. She will choose between basketball, hockey, swimming, and volleyball. To help her decide, Janet asks her family and friends to each vote for one of the sports listed above. Janet made the circle graph to the right to show the results.

Sports

---

1. Which sport received the most votes?

   _____

2. Which two sports appear to have received an equal number of votes?

   _____

3. Janet will also choose from the following after-school activities: math club, the newspaper, and student council. Draw a tree diagram to show the number of possible outcomes from choosing 1 of the 4 sports and 1 of the 3 activities. How many outcomes are possible?

   _____ outcomes

4. Based only on the tree diagram, what is the probability that Janet will choose math club and either swimming or hockey?

   _____

5. Janet decides to play basketball. During the season, she scores the following number of points in the first 5 games: 19, 24, 14, 30, and 16. What is the range of this data?

   _____ points

6. Use the number of points Janet scores each game to create a stem-and-leaf plot.

   19, 24, 14, 30, 16

Lesson 11.1 Reading Bar Graphs

Read the problem carefully and solve. Show your work under each question.

Jordan and Nick made the bar graph to the right. The graph shows the number of miles they each rode their bike for the last six days.

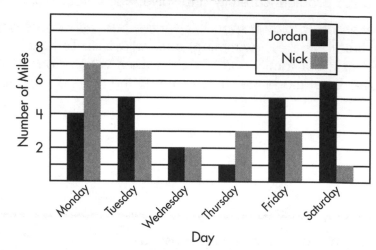

Number of Miles Biked

Helpful Hint

A **double-bar graph** shows two sets of information on one bar graph. This is useful for comparing the two sets.

1. On which day did Jordan and Nick each ride the same number of miles?

_____

2. Who rode more miles on Friday?

_____

3. How many miles did Nick ride on Monday?

_____ miles

4. How many miles altogether did Jordan and Nick ride on Tuesday?

_____ miles

5. How many total miles did Jordan ride her bike during the six days?

_____ miles

Lesson 11.2 Reading Line Graphs

Read the problem carefully and solve. Show your work under each question.

Amy and Tyrone are both raising money for the school's sports teams. The line graph on the right shows how much money they each raised from Monday to Friday this week.

Money Raised for School Sports

Helpful Hint

A **double-line graph** shows two sets of information on one line graph. In this example, each line represents the amount of money one of the students collected.

1. On Monday, who collected the most money?

_____

2. On which day was the difference between the amounts of money they each collected the greatest?

_____

3. On which days did Tyrone have less money raised than Amy?

_____ and

_____

4. On which day did Amy bring in the least amount of money?

_____

5. How much money altogether did both students raise during the week?

_____

Lesson 11.3 Reading Circle Graphs

Read the problem carefully and solve. Show your work under each question.

The bakery downtown sells four different types of pies: apple, cherry, pecan, and pumpkin. The circle graph on the right shows the pies sold this week. The bakery sold a total of 40 pies this week.

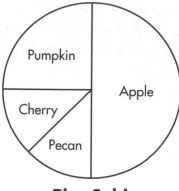

Pies Sold

Helpful Hint

A **circle graph** shows the relationship between parts of a group. The circle represents the whole group and the sections represent the parts of the group.

1. What type of pie was sold the most often this week?

_____

2. How many cherry pies were sold this week?

_____

3. How many pumpkin pies were sold this week?

_____

4. Apple pies sell for $8 each. How much money was made from selling apple pies?

_____

5. Pecan pies sell for $12 each. How much money was made from selling pecan pies?

_____

Lesson 11.4 Measures of Central Tendency

Read the problem carefully and solve. Show your work under each question. Round all numbers to the nearest whole number.

Every year, Jerome goes on an 8-day camping trip with his dad to a state park. Each year, Jerome keeps track of the number of hawks he sees and records the data. Jerome always rounds his answers to the nearest tenth. His results for this year are 5, 12, 8, 0, 1, 7, 5, and 6.

Helpful Hint

The **mean** is the average of a set of numbers.

The **median** is the middle number of a set of numbers. If there are two middle numbers, the median is the average of the two.

The **mode** is the number that appears the most often in a set of numbers.

The **range** is the difference between the greatest and the least number of the set.

---

1. Jerome wants to calculate the mean number of hawks that he saw on his trip this year. What is the mean?

_____

2. What are the mode and range of Jerome's data?

mode: _____ range: _____

3. What is the median of Jerome's data?

_____

4. If Jerome stayed another day and saw 14 more hawks, how would this affect all four measures of central tendency?

mean _____   median _____

mode _____   range _____

5. The list below shows Jerome's data from last year. Compare it to this year's data. Which measure of central tendency changed the most? By how much did it change?

4, 5, 11, 6, 1, 5, 0, 2

_____

_____

Lesson 11.5 Stem-and-Leaf Plots

Read the problem carefully and solve. Show your work under each question.

Ms. Washington teaches math. She compiles the final grades for her students for this semester. Each student has taken 8 math tests. Ms. Washington wants to record these test grades in stem-and-leaf plots.

Helpful Hint

In a **stem-and-leaf plot**, the place value of the stems and the leaves are shown in the Key.

Example:

The data set 11, 12, 14, 18, 22, and 26 in a stem-and-leaf plot:

Stem	Leaves
1	1 2 4 8
2	2 6

Key: 1 | 4 = 14

1. Claudia's scores are shown below. Create a stem-and-leaf plot for the set of data.

79, 92, 81, 85, 68, 88, 71, 93

2. Raul's scores are shown below. Create a stem-and-leaf plot for the set of data.

95, 92, 65, 81, 84, 92, 68, 81

3. Derek's scores are shown below. Create a stem-and-leaf plot for the set of data.

78, 86, 80, 78, 75, 88, 70, 87

4. Andrea's scores are shown below. Create a stem-and-leaf plot for the set of data.

80, 81, 80, 98, 94, 78, 76, 86

5. Which student had the most scores of 90 or more?

_____

Lesson 11.6 Box-and-Whisker Plots

Read the problem carefully and solve. Show your work under each question.

Each of Ms. Washington's students has taken 7 quizzes. The quizzes are graded out of a total of 40 points. Raul's scores were 10, 15, 25, 25, 30, 30, and 40.

Helpful Hint

Box-and-whisker plots are helpful in interpreting the distribution of data. For example, the results of a test might include these 15 scores:

66, 56, 75, 77, 98, 72, 48, 83, 73, 89, 65, 74, 87, 85, 81

The numbers should be arranged in order:

48, 56, 65, 66, 72, 73, 74, 75, 77, 81, 83, 85, 87, 89, 98

The median is 75. The lower quartile is the median of the lower half (66). The upper quartile is the median of the upper half (85). Draw a box around the median with its ends going through the quartiles. Each quartile contains one-fourth of the scores.

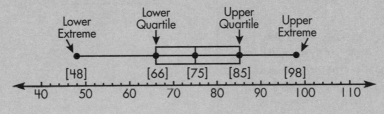

1. What is the median of Raul's scores?

   _____

2. What is the lower quartile of Raul's scores?

   _____

3. What is the upper quartile of Raul's scores?

   _____

4. Using the number line below, draw a box-and-whisker plot for Raul's scores.

   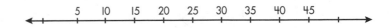

5. Andrea's scores on the quiz were 5, 15, 20, 25, 35, 35, and 40. Draw a box-and-whisker plot showing this data on the number line below.

   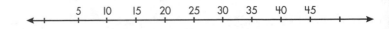

Lesson 11.7 Making Tree Diagrams and Calculating Probability

Read the problem carefully and solve. Show your work under each question.

Deb flips a coin and spins a spinner. She wants to find the probability of the coin landing on heads twice in a row. She also wants to find the probability of the spinner on the right landing on an odd number twice in a row.

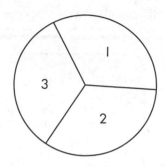

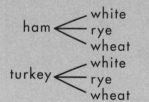

Helpful Hint

A **tree diagram** is useful to find the number of possible combinations. The **probability** of an event is the measure of how likely the event will occur.

	white	ham on white bread
ham	rye	ham on rye bread
	wheat	ham on wheat bread
	white	turkey on white bread
turkey	rye	turkey on rye bread
	wheat	turkey on wheat bread

1. If Deb spins the spinner once, what is the probability that the spinner will land on an even number?

   _____

2. Deb flips the coin 2 times. Draw a tree diagram to show the number of possible outcomes.

3. Based on the tree diagram for flipping the coin twice, what is the probability that the coin will land on heads both times?

   _____

4. Deb spins the spinner twice. Draw a tree diagram that shows how many possible outcomes there are.

5. What is the probability that the spinner will land on an odd number twice in a row?

   _____

NAME_____

Check What You Learned

Probability and Statistics

Read the problem carefully and solve. Show your work under each question.

Lucas and Jamal play a trivia game where each correct answer receives 5 points. They keep track of the total number of points they each score through 6 rounds of the game. This data is on the line graph to the right.

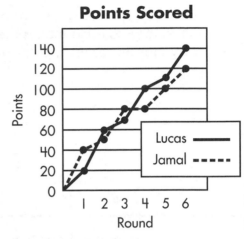

Points Scored

CHAPTER 11 POSTTEST

1. After 1 round, how many more points did Jamal have than Lucas?

_____

2. Who scored the most points during the 6 rounds?

_____

3. Jamal's points during each round are 40, 10, 30, 0, 20, and 20. What is the range of this data?

_____

4. The data set below shows the scores of each player for each round. What is the upper quartile for this data?

0, 10, 10, 10, 20, 20, 20, 30, 30, 30, 40, 40

_____

5. Using the number line below, draw a box-and-whisker plot showing the data set in the previous question.

6. In the final round, each player reaches into a bag and chooses a card. Each card has a final trivia question. There are 30 cards to choose from. Six of the cards have a question about science. What is the probability of choosing a science question?

_____

Check What You Learned

Probability and Statistics

Read the problem carefully and solve. Show your work under each question.

Steve has a jar of marbles. There are three colors of marbles in the jar: red, blue, and green. He makes the circle graph to the right to show how many marbles of each color are in the jar.

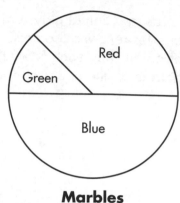

Marbles

1. Which color marble does Steve have the most of in the jar?

   _____

2. Which color marble does Steve have the least of in the jar?

   _____

3. Draw a tree diagram to show how many outcomes there will be from choosing 2 marbles from the jar.

4. Based only on the tree diagram, what is the probability that Steve will pick 1 red marble and 1 blue marble?

   _____

5. Steve also has a second jar of marbles. This jar has 17 red marbles, 33 green marbles, 26 blue marbles, 14 purple marbles, and 20 yellow marbles. What is the mean of this data?

   _____

6. Use the number of different color of marbles in the second jar to create a stem-and-leaf plot.

   17, 33, 26, 14, 20

Check What You Know

Geometry

Read the problem carefully and solve. Show your work under each question.

Carlos and Olivia make a poster. They decorate the poster with different types of shapes and lines.

1. Carlos draws the solid figure below onto his poster. Name the figure. Write the number of faces and vertices it has.

Name: _____

Number of faces: _____

Number of vertices: _____

2. Olivia draws the triangle below. Identify this triangle as acute, right, or obtuse.

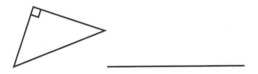 _____

3. Carlos draws a ray. Draw ray *AB* below.

4. Olivia draws the two quadrilaterals shown below. Name the polygons and identify them as congruent or not congruent.

Each polygon is called a

_____.

The polygons are

_____.

5. Carlos draws a circle. Then, he draws a line segment in the circle. Identify this line segment as a radius, chord, or diameter.

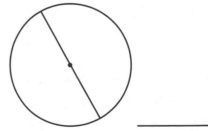 _____

Lesson 12.1 Points, Lines, Rays and Measuring Angles

Read the problem carefully and solve. Show your work under each question.

Dennis plans to remodel his backyard. He draws a model of the yard on graph paper. He labels his drawing and uses a ruler to make straight lines.

Helpful Hints

A **point** is named by a capital letter.

A **line** is named by choosing any two points on it. $\overleftrightarrow{AB}$ can also be written as $\overleftrightarrow{BA}$.

A **line segment** is named by its two endpoints. $\overline{DE}$ can also be written as $\overline{ED}$.

A **ray** is always named starting with its endpoint. $\overrightarrow{CD}$ cannot be written as $\overrightarrow{DC}$.

An **angle** is formed from two rays with a common vertex. A **right angle** measures 90°. An **acute angle** measures less than 90°. An **obtuse angle** measures greater than 90°.

1. Dennis wants to put a pool in his backyard. He draws a line segment to show one side of the pool. Draw and name line segment CD below.

2. Dennis draws the figure below. Identify and name this figure.

_____ _____

3. Dennis draws a right angle to show a corner of his yard. He names the angle LJK. Draw and label ∠LJK in the space below.

4. Dennis draws the angle below to show a part of his patio. Name the angle, and write whether it is obtuse, acute, or right. Then, measure the angle.

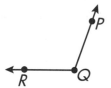

_____ _____ _____

5. Dennis draws the angle below to show a part of his garden. Name the angle, and write whether it is obtuse, acute, or right. Then, measure the angle.

_____ _____ _____

Lesson 12.2 Types of Angles

Read the problem carefully and solve. Show your work under each question.

Keisha makes a map of the streets near her house. She uses angles and intersecting lines to represent the streets. She decides to label the lines and angles on her map. She also plans to measure some of the angles.

Helpful Hints

Vertical angles are formed when two straight lines intersect. They are opposite angles and are equal.

Two angles are **supplementary** if their sum is 180°.

Two angles are **complementary** if their sum is 90°.

An **angle bisector** is a line drawn through the vertex of an angle that divides it into two angles that have the same measure.

Use the figure below for questions 1 and 2.

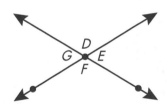

1. Keisha draws the pair of lines above to show the intersection of two streets. Identify ∠D and ∠F as supplementary, complementary, or vertical.

   _____

2. In Keisha's drawing above, identify ∠F and ∠G as supplementary, complementary, or vertical.

   _____

3. Keisha measures two complementary angles, ∠B and ∠C, on her map. The measure of ∠B is 35°. What is the measure of ∠C?

   _____

4. Keisha measures two supplementary angles, ∠J and ∠K, on her map. The measure of ∠K is 124°. What is the measure of ∠J?

   _____

5. Keisha draws ∠RST below. She draws $\overline{SV}$ so that it bisects ∠RST. The measure of ∠VST is 25°. What is the measure of ∠RST?

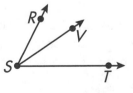

   _____

Lesson 12.3 Triangles

Read the problem carefully and solve. Show your work under each question.

Bonnie makes earrings to sell at her jewerly store. She likes to make earrings out of different shapes. This month, she decides to make earrings in the shape of triangles. She plans to use three different types of triangles.

Helpful Hints

Triangles have three sides. The sum of the angle measures in a triangle always equals 180°.

1. **Acute triangles** have three angles that measure less than 90°.

2. **Right triangles** have one right angle. Right angles measure 90°.

3. **Obtuse triangles** have one angle that measures greater than 90°.

4. The area of a triangle is found by the formula $\frac{1}{2} \times$ base $\times$ height.

1. Bonnie makes her first pair of earrings. Each earring is shaped like the triangle below. Identify this triangle as acute, right, or obtuse.

2. Bonnie makes another pair of earrings. Each earring is shaped like the triangle below. What is the area of the triangle?

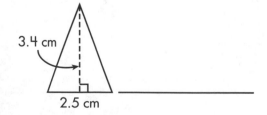

3. Bonnie has a sale on one type of triangular earring. Each earring that is on sale is shaped like the triangle below. Identify this triangle as acute, right, or obtuse.

4. Bonnie makes another pair of earrings. Each earring is shaped like the triangle below. What is the area of the triangle?

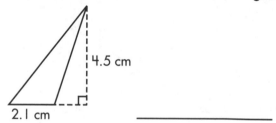

5. Bonnie runs out of one type of earring shaped like the triangle below. Identify this triangle as acute, right, or obtuse.

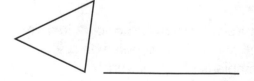

Lesson 12.4 Quadrilaterals and Polygons

Read the problem carefully and solve. Show your work under each question.

Joanne and Natalia make a quilt with seven different types of polygons cut out of cloth. Before they start, they sort the polygons below in a variety of ways. They give each type of polygon a letter to make the sorting easier.

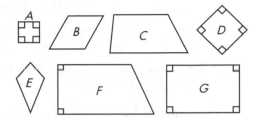

Helpful Hint

A **rectangle** has four right angles, two pairs of parallel sides, and two pairs of congruent sides.

A **square** is a rectangle with four congruent sides. It is also a special kind of rhombus.

A **rhombus** has two pairs of parallel sides and four congruent sides.

A **trapezoid** has exactly one pair of parallel sides.

A **kite** has two pairs of congruent sides but no parallel sides.

Two polygons are called **congruent** if they are exactly the same size and shape. Their corresponding sides and corresponding angles must be congruent.

Volume can be found by multiplying length × width × height.

1. Natalia sorts all the polygons to find the ones that are rectangles. Write the letters of the polygons that are rectangles.

_____

2. Joanne sorts all the polygons to find the ones that are trapezoids. Write the letters of the polygons that are trapezoids.

_____

3. Natalia puts some of the cloth in a storage container. What is the volume of the container?

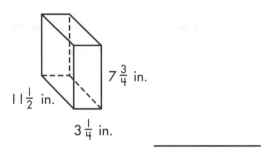

$7\frac{3}{4}$ in.

$11\frac{1}{2}$ in.

$3\frac{1}{4}$ in.

_____

4. Natalia cuts out the two polygons below from purple cloth. Name the polygons and identify them as congruent or not congruent.

Each polygon is called a _____.

The polygons are _____.

5. Joanne cuts out the two polygons below from red cloth. Identify the polygons as congruent or not congruent.

_____

Lesson 12.5 Polygons in the Coordinate Plane

Read the problem carefully and solve.
Show your work under each question.

The distance from the museum to the community hall is 8 miles. These buildings have the same *y* coordinate. The distance between −5 and +3 is 8 miles.

The 3 locations form a triangle.

Area of a triangle $= \frac{1}{2}bh$

$\qquad\qquad = \frac{1}{2} \times 8$ miles $\times 8$ miles

$\qquad\qquad = 32$ miles^2

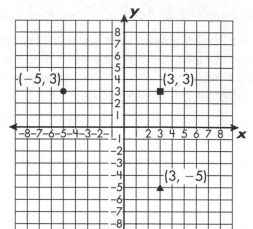

● museum
■ community hall
▲ nursing college

1 point = 1 mile

Use this graph to solve the problems:

1. Plot the locations of the school, office, and park on the graph.

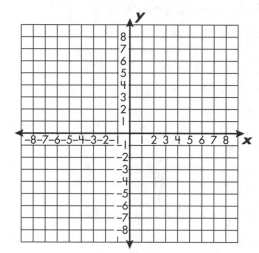

● school (−1, 1)
■ office (4, 1)
▲ park (4, −4)

1 point = 1 mile

2. The 3 locations form what shape?

_____

3. What is the distance from the school to the office? Answer in ordered pairs.

_____

4. What is the difference in position between the school and the office? They share the same *y* coordinate.

_____ miles

5. What is the area of the shape in problem 2?

_____ miles^2

Lesson 12.6 Circles

Read the problem carefully and solve. Show your work under each question.

Carolyn designs sets of circular coasters. First, she draws a diagram of her design in pencil. Then, she labels her drawing using letters. The circle to the right shows Carolyn's design.

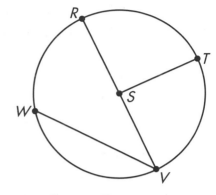

Helpful Hint

The **origin** of a circle is the center point inside the circle. A circle is named by its origin.

A **radius** of a circle is a line segment with one endpoint at the origin and the other endpoint on the circle.

A **chord** is a line segment with both endpoints on the circle.

A **diameter** is a chord that passes through the origin of the circle.

1. Name a diameter in Carolyn's circle design. If there is more than one, list them all.

_____

2. Name a radius in the circle. If there is more than one, list them all.

_____

3. Name a chord in Carolyn's circle that is not a diameter.

_____

4. Name the origin of the circle.

_____

5. Carolyn starts another circle design for a new set of coasters. She draws a line segment in the circle below. Identify this line segment as a radius, chord, or diameter.

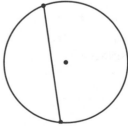

_____

Lesson 12.7 Solid Figures

Read the problem carefully and solve. Show your work under each question.

Masako plans to use the solid figures below in a model that he will build for a school project. Before he starts, he decides to keep track of the number of faces, vertices, and edges for each solid.

triangular pyramid

cone

triangular solid

rectangular solid

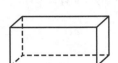
square pyramid

cylinder

3. How many more edges does a square pyramid have than a triangular pyramid?

_____

Helpful Hint

A **face** is a flat surface of a solid figure.

An **edge** is the intersection of two faces.

A **vertex** is a point where three or more faces meet.

A **base** is a face on which a solid figure rests.

1. Which of Masako's solids has the largest number of vertices? How many does it have?

_____

_____

4. One of Masako's solids has no vertices. Which one is it?

_____

2. Masako notices that two of the solids have the same number of faces. What are these two solids?

_____

_____

5. The first shape Masako is going to use in his model has only one vertex and a circular base. What is the name of this solid?

_____

Check What You Learned

Geometry

Read the problem carefully and solve. Show your work under each question.

Masako continues to build his model for his school project. He decides to use polygons and circles as well as solid figures in his model.

1. Masako uses the solid figure below in his model. Name the figure. Write the number of faces and vertices it has.

   Name: _____

   Number of faces: _____

   Number of vertices: _____

2. Masako draws the triangle below. Identify this triangle as acute, right, or obtuse.

3. Masako starts to draw another polygon. He draws a line segment first. Draw line segment *RS* in the space below.

4. Masako draws a line segment in the circle. Identify this line segment as a radius, chord, or diameter in the circle below.

   _____

5. Masako draws the two quadrilaterals below. Name the polygons and identify them as congruent or not congruent.

   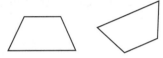

   Each polygon is called a

   _____.

   The polygons are _____.

6. Masako draws the figure below. Identify ∠X and ∠Y as complementary, vertical, or supplementary angles. Solve for the measure of ∠X if ∠Y = 38°.

   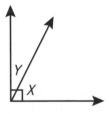

   ∠X and ∠Y are _____ angles.

   ∠X measures _____.

NAME _____

Check What You Know

Preparing for Algebra

Read the problem carefully and solve. Show your work under each question.

Isaac owns a math-themed store. The store has many math-inspired souvenirs and games for sale. Isaac put expressions and equations on the price tags of all the items to show the prices in dollars.

1. The store has a mug for sale that has drawings of different shapes on the side. The price tag shows the expression $12 - 3 \times 2$. What is the value of the expression?

_____

2. The cost of a calculator is shown by the expression $(6 \times 1) + (6 \times 2)$. Rewrite the expression using the distributive property.

_____

3. Isaac's store sells a calendar that has a different solid figure shown each month. The price tag shows the expression $(8 + 3) + 4$. Use the associative property to rewrite the expression.

_____

4. Isaac wants to write the price of a math board game as an algebraic equation. He wants the equation to say "the product of n and 5 is 25." Write the equation.

_____

5. A T-shirt with a picture of a parallelogram on it costs p. Isaac wrote the equation below. What is the value of p?

$$p + 7 = 19$$

$p =$ _____

6. A puzzle cube costs c. Isaac wrote the equation below. What is the value of c?

$$\frac{c}{8} = 3$$

$c =$ _____

Check What You Know

Preparing for Algebra

Read the problem carefully and solve. Show your work under each question.

Isaac counts the number of souvenirs and games he has sold during the month. He wants to compare the numbers to find how many of each item he should order for the upcoming month.

1. Isaac found that the number of souvenir pencils he sold is equal to 7^4. Write this power as a product of factors.

_____

2. Isaac represents items he has sold as negative integers and items he has in stock at the store as positive numbers. Use > or < to compare the numbers below.

-7 _____ 4

3. Isaac lists the number of different jigsaw puzzles in his store as the following integers: $-6, 5, -2, -3,$ and 2. List these integers in order from smallest to largest.

_____

4. Isaac calculates the change in the number of T-shirts in the store as the expression below. What is the value of the expression?

$$-4 + (7)$$

_____

5. Isaac calculates the change in the number of calculators in the store as the expression below. What is the value of the expression?

$$-3 + (-5)$$

_____

6. Isaac wants to plot the point G on a grid at $(4, 5)$ to show that he sold 5 games on the fourth day of the month. Plot the point on the grid below.

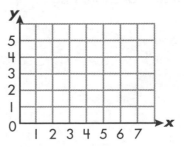

Lesson 13.1 The Order of Operations

Read the problem carefully and solve. Show your work under each question.

Julia and Sheila work at a bakery. As a fun game, Sheila writes mathematic expressions to show how many of each baked item Julia should bake. Julia must solve each of these expressions.

Helpful Hint

The **order of operations**:

1. All operations within parentheses

2. All exponents

3. All multiplication and division, from left to right

4. All addition and subtraction, from left to right

1. The expression below shows how many rolls Julia should bake. Name the operation that should be completed first.

$$12 \div 3 \times 5$$

_____

2. The expression below shows how many bagels Julia should bake. Name the operation that should be completed first.

$$(2 + 5) \times 3$$

_____

3. Sheila wrote the expression below to show how many bran muffins Julia should bake. What is the value of the expression?

$$15 \div 3 + 16 \div 4$$

_____

4. Sheila wrote the expression below to show how many loaves of bread Julia should bake. What is the value of the expression?

$$(7 - 3) \times 2$$

_____

5. Julia must solve the expression below to find how many birthday cakes to bake today. What is the value of the expression?

$$84 \div (8 + 6) \div 3$$

_____

NAME

Lesson 13.2 Number Properties

Read the problem carefully and solve. Show your work under each question.

Julia now makes expressions for Sheila to solve. The expressions are based on the amount of the ingredients they use at the bakery. She wants Sheila to rewrite each expression based on the commutative, associative, and distributive properties.

Helpful Hint

Commutative Properties of addition and multiplication:
$a + b = b + a$
$a \times b = b \times a$

Associative Properties of addition and multiplication:
$(a + b) + c = a + (b + c)$
$(a \times b) \times c = a \times (b \times c)$

Distributive Property:
$a \times (b + c) = (a \times b) + (a \times c)$

1. Julia wrote the expression below to show how many gallons of milk Sheila needs for a recipe. Rewrite the expression using the commutative property.

$$4 \times 3$$

2. Julia wrote the expression below to show how many cups of sugar Sheila needs for a recipe. Rewrite the expression using the associative property.

$$(2 + 5) + 4$$

3. Julia wrote the expression below to show how many cups of flour Sheila needs for a recipe. Use the distributive property to write an equivalent expression.

$$4 \times (6 + 2)$$

4. The expression below shows how many muffin pans Sheila needs to bake bran muffins. Rewrite the expression using the associative property.

$$(1 \times 4) \times 2$$

5. The expression below shows how many sticks of butter Sheila needs for a recipe. Use the distributive property to write an equivalent expression.

$$(5 \times 1) + (5 \times 6)$$

Lesson 13.3 Variable Expressions and Equations

Read the problem carefully and solve. Show your work under each question.

Chen writes expressions on the chalkboard for his teacher, Mr. Walsh.

Helpful Hints

A **variable** is a symbol that stands for an unknown number. Example: a

An **algebraic expression** is a combination of numbers, variables, and operations.
Example: $x + 13$

Factors are numbers you can multiply together to get an expression.

A **term** is a number, variable, product, or quotient in an algebraic expression.
Example: $3a + 5$

A **coefficient** is a number that multiplies a variable. Example: $3a$

An **equation** is a sentence with an equal sign. Example: $x + 13 = 25$

1. Chen writes $3 + x$. Is this an expression or equation?

_____

2. Chen writes $x - 7 = 15$. Is this an expression or equation?

_____

3. Chen wrote the term $7b$ on the chalkboard. Identify the coefficient and the variable.

coefficient _____ variable _____

4. Mr. Walsh asks Chen to write "seven more than x" on the board. Translate the phrase into an algebraic expression.

_____

5. Mr. Walsh asks Chen to write "the product of y and 12 equals 84" on the board. Write the equation.

_____

Lesson 13.4 Solving Addition and Subtraction Equations

Read the problem carefully and solve. Show your work under each question.

Kelley keeps track of her spending. Each time she leaves the house, she counts her money. When she returns, she counts her money again.

Helpful Hint

Add or subtract the same amount from both sides of an equation to solve.

Examples:

$$x + 12 = 20$$
$$x + 12 - 12 = 20 - 12$$
$$x = 8$$
$$t - 6 = 10$$
$$t - 6 + 6 = 10 + 6$$
$$t = 16$$

1. The equation below shows how much Kelley spent on Monday. What operation would undo the operation in the equation?

$$f + 22 = 30$$

_____

2. Kelley spent $4 on Tuesday. She had $12 when she returned home. The equation below shows how much Kelley had before she left on Tuesday. What operation would undo the operation in the equation?

$$g - 4 = 12$$

_____

3. On Wednesday, Kelley went to the movies with $30 and returned with $22. Solve the equation below to show how much she spent.

$$x + 22 = 30$$

$x =$ _____

4. On Thursday, Kelley spent $7 on a birthday present for her mother. She had $17 when she returned. Solve the equation below to find how much money Kelley had originally.

$$d - 7 = 17$$

$d =$ _____

5. To start the week, Kelley had $82. She now has $32. She wrote the equation below to find how much money she spent. Solve the equation.

$$a + 32 = 82$$

$a =$ _____

Lesson 13.5 Solving Multiplication and Division Equations

Read the problem carefully and solve. Show your work under each question.

Chris works as a carpenter. He buys long boards of wood from the lumber yard. He then cuts the boards into different lengths to use for building.

Helpful Hint

Multiply or divide each side of an equation by the same amount to solve.

Examples:

$3 \times y = 21$ $\frac{a}{4} = 5$

divide by 3 to undo   multiply by 4 to undo

$\frac{3 \times y}{3} = \frac{21}{3}$ $\frac{a}{4} \times \frac{4}{1} = 5 \times 4$

$y = 7$ $a = 20$

1. Chris plans to cut a board into 3 sections that are each 4 feet long. Chris wrote the equation below to show this situation. Write the operation that will undo the operation in the equation.

$$\frac{c}{3} = 4$$

_____

2. Chris bought 5 pieces of wood. Altogether, the wood measures a total of 30 feet. Write the operation that will undo the operation in the equation below.

$$5 \times b = 30$$

_____

3. Chris cuts a piece of wood that is d feet long into pieces that are 8 feet long. There are 3 pieces when Chris is finished cutting. Solve the equation below to find the original length of the wood.

$$\frac{d}{3} = 8$$

$d =$ _____

4. Chris cuts a piece of wood that is 16 feet long into pieces that are each 2 feet long. Solve the equation below to find how many pieces of wood Chris cuts.

$$2 \times p = 16$$

$p =$ _____

5. Chris cuts a piece of wood that is x feet long into 4 pieces that are each 5 feet long. Solve the equation below to find the length of the piece of wood.

$$\frac{x}{5} = 4$$

$x =$ _____

Lesson 13.6 Expressions and Equations

Read the problem carefully and solve. Show your work under each question.

The skating rink charges $100 to reserve the rink, and then $5 per person. Write an expression to represent the cost for any number of people.

n = the number of people

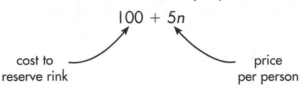

$$100 + 5n$$

cost to
reserve rink

price
per person

---

1. Maria has three more than twice as many pens as Liz. Write an expression to represent the number of pens Maria has.

   _____

2. An amusement park charges $28 to enter and $0.35 per ticket for rides. Write an expression to represent the total amount spent.

   _____

3. Drew has a job doing yard work. He is paid $15 per hour and a $20 bonus when he completes a yard. Write an equation to represent the amount of money he earned after completing one yard.

   _____

4. Santo made 4 less than twice as many cupcakes as Lynn. Write an equation to represent the number of cupcakes that Santo made.

   _____

5. Tom earned $5 mowing the lawn on Saturday. He earned more money on Sunday. Write an equation that shows the amount of money Tom has earned.

   _____

6. Describe a problem situation that can be solved using the equation $2c + 3 = 15$ where c represents the cost of an item.

   _____

   _____

   _____

NAME_____

Lesson 13.7 Inequalities

Read the problem carefully and solve. Show your work under each question.

An inequality states that values are not equal.

The Flores family spent less than $200 on groceries last month. The inequality 200 > x represents this, where x is the amount spent on groceries.

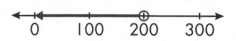

Symbol	Meaning
>	greater than
<	less than
≥	greater than or equal to
≤	less than or equal to

3. Mike's class spent less than $250 on their field trip last year. Write an inequality to represent this, where y is the amount spent.

_____

Helpful Hint

An open circle is used when an inequality contains a < or > symbol to show solutions that are less than or greater than, but not equal to, a number.

1. Jan's class must raise at least $100 to go on a field trip. They have collected $20. Write an inequality to represent the amount of money, m, the class still needs to raise.

_____

4. Represent the inequality you wrote in question 3 on the number line.

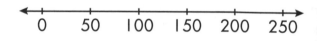

2. Represent the inequality you wrote in question 1 on the number line.

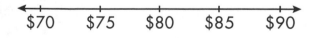

5. What inequality does the number line show? Write your answer starting with x.

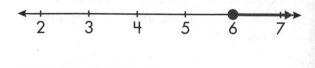

_____

Lesson 13.8 Exponents and Scientific Notation

Read the problem carefully and solve. Show your work under each question.

Brett researches the United States for a geography report. He uses exponents and scientific notation to represent large numbers in the report. He checked out several large books from the school library to help with his report.

Helpful Hint

Scientific notation for a number is written as a number between 1 and 10, not including 10, multiplied by a power of ten.

$10^1 = 10$

$10^2 = 10 \times 10 = 100$

$10^3 = 10 \times 10 \times 10 = 1,000$

$10^4 = 10 \times 10 \times 10 \times 10 = 10,000$

$10^5 = 10 \times 10 \times 10 \times 10 \times 10 = 100,000$

1. Brett writes that New York and San Diego are about 4,000 kilometers apart. Write this number in scientific notation.

   _____

2. Brett writes that Chicago and St. Louis are about 400 kilometers apart. Write this number in scientific notation.

   _____

3. One of the books Brett uses for his research has 12^2 pages. Write the power as a product of factors.

   _____

4. Another of the books that Brett checks out has the number of pages shown by the expression below. Write the expression as an exponent.

   $$5 \times 5 \times 5 \times 5$$

   _____

5. Mr. Glenn, Brett's geography teacher, collected all of the students' reports on Friday. The total number of pages the students turned in can be shown by the expression p^3. What is the value of this expression if $p = 4$?

   _____

Lesson 13.9 Absolute Value

Read the problem carefully and solve. Show your work under each question.

Absolute values are the size or magnitude of a number. $|x|$, or the absolute value of x, is the distance away from 0, and is always positive or 0. The absolute value of -6 and 6 is 6.

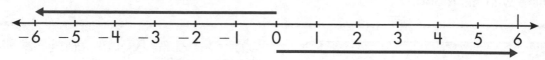

Helpful Hint

The absolute value of a number is its distance from zero.

1. What is the absolute value of -27?

   _____

2. Sam has -150 dollars in his account. How would you express the amount of his debt in dollars using absolute value?

   _____

3. Sam and his friend Jack were looking at their debts. Jack has $144 of debt and Sam has $150 of debt. Who owes more money?

   _____

4. Spencer ran 63 miles last week. He needed to run 75 miles. How would you express the deficit of the amount of miles he ran, -12, using absolute value?

   _____

5. Randy wanted to get 56 hours of sleep last week. He only slept 42 hours. How would you express the deficit of the amount of sleep he got, -14, using absolute value?

   _____

6. Last week, Brad had $15. Over the weekend, he received $25 for gardening. How much money does he have now? Express your answer in absolute value.

   _____

Lesson 13.10 Comparing and Ordering Integers

Read the problem carefully and solve. Show your work under each question.

Janelle wrote the number line below to show the temperature in Celsius of her hometown during 6 days this winter. She marked each day with a letter to show the high temperature for that day, starting with A for *Monday* through F for *Saturday*.

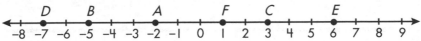

Helpful Hint

Positive integers are greater than 0. **Negative integers** are less than 0. On a number line, the smaller of two integers is always to the left of the larger integer.

1. The temperature on Saturday is shown by the letter *F*. Use an integer to name that point on the number line.

   _____

2. The temperature on Wednesday is shown by the letter *C*. Use an integer to name that point on the number line.

   _____

3. The temperatures on Monday and Tuesday were -2°C and -5°C. Use either $>$ or $<$ to compare these temperatures.

   -2 _____ -5

4. The temperatures on Thursday and Friday were -7°C and 6°C. Use either $>$ or $<$ to compare these temperatures.

   -7 _____ 6

5. Janelle wrote down the temperatures for 4 more days. The integers for those temperatures are below. List the integers in order from smallest to largest.

   $0, 5, -3, -7$

   _____

Lesson 13.11 Adding Integers

Read the problem carefully and solve. Show your work under each question.

Kim keeps track of the money that she earns and spends this month. She deposits any money she makes into her bank account and withdraws any money she spends from the same account. The money she earns is shown as positive integers and the money she spends is shown as negative integers.

Helpful Hint

To add two integers, start at zero and move along a number line by the values of the integers.

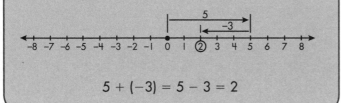

$$5 + (-3) = 5 - 3 = 2$$

1. Kim made $6 by mowing the lawn and $2 by recycling cans. She deposited all this money into her account. Solve the expression below representing this situation.

$$6 + 2$$

_____

2. Kim spent $3 from her account on a necklace and $4 on a pair of earrings. Solve the expression below representing this situation.

$$(-3) + (-4)$$

_____

3. Kim earned $5 for doing chores and spent $2 on a bottle of fruit juice. Solve the expression below representing this situation.

$$5 + (-2)$$

_____

4. Kim spent $9 on a new shirt. That same day, she made $4 for helping her friend paint. Solve the expression below representing this situation.

$$-9 + 4$$

_____

5. Kim spent $6 on school supplies and $4 on a bus pass. Solve the expression below representing this situation.

$$-6 + (-4)$$

_____

Lesson 13.12 Integers

Read the problem carefully and solve. Show your work under each question.

Integers are the set of whole numbers and their opposites. Two integers are opposites if they are the same distance away from zero, but on opposite sides of the number line.

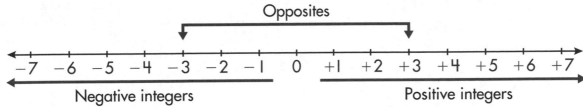

Opposites

Negative integers   Positive integers

Keiko is on vacation in the mountains.

1. Keiko takes a helicopter from 10 feet below sea level to 10 feet above sea level. Express these integers using negative and positive signs.

   _____

   Are these integers opposites?

   _____

2. At Keiko's cabin in the mountains, it was −14°F when she woke up. In the afternoon, it was 14°F. Are −14 and 14 opposite integers?

   _____

3. The next day, the high temperature is 18°F. What is the opposite of 18?

   _____

4. From 400 meters above sea level, Keiko took a helicopter and landed 800 meters above sea level. What integer represents Keiko's change in altitude?

   _____ meters

5. When her helicopter lands, it's −20°F. When Keiko returns to her cabin that afternoon, it's 20°F. Are −20 and 20 opposites?

   _____

   Graph −20 and 20 on the number line.

   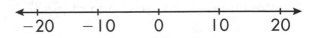

Lesson 13.13 Plotting Ordered Pairs

Read the problem carefully and solve. Show your work under each question.

Lee graphed and labeled 10 points on the grid to the right.

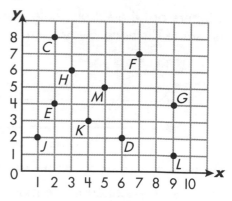

Helpful Hint

Points on a grid are located based on their (x, y) coordinates. The horizontal number is x and the vertical number is y. Point A on the grid below is at (3, 2) which is 3 to the right and 2 up from the origin. Point B is at (7, 3).

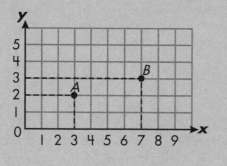

1. Which point did Lee graph at (6, 2)?

_____

2. Which point did Lee graph at (4, 3)?

_____

3. Find the ordered pair for point M.

_____

4. Find the ordered pair for point G.

_____

5. Lee wants to plot point A on his graph at (5, 1). Plot this point on the graph below.

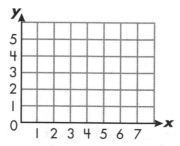

Lesson 13.14 Coordinate Planes

Read the problem carefully and solve. Show your work under each question.

Beth draws a coordinate plane to help her design a mural she is painting.

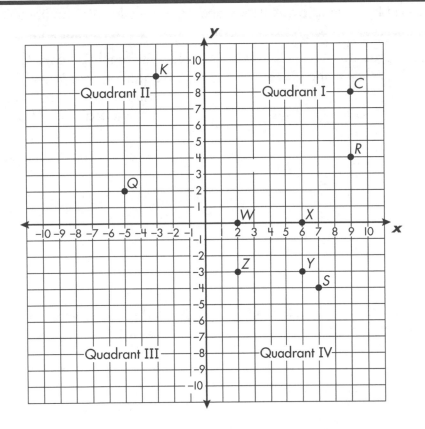

1. Beth paints a tree at $(-3, 4)$. In which Quadrant is $(-3, 4)$?

    _____

2. Beth paints a sunflower at the spot that is marked with the letter S. Which ordered pair represents point S?

    _____

3. Beth paints a cloud at $(9, 8)$. Which letter represents this point?

    _____

4. Beth paints a garden in the rectangle marked ZWXY. Graph the image of rectangle ZWXY over the x-axis.

    _____

5. Beth paints a kite at point $(-3, 9)$. Graph this point and label it point K.

    _____

6. What is the distance between point C and point R?

    _____

Check What You Learned

Preparing for Algebra

Read the problem carefully and solve. Show your work under each question.

Claire earns extra credit by writing expressions and equations for Ms. Smithson's math class.

1. Claire writes the expression $(4 \times 3) + (5 \times 2)$. What is the value of the expression?

_____

2. Claire writes the expression $4 \times (5 + 9)$. Rewrite this expression using the distributive property.

_____

3. Claire writes the expression $4 \times (3 \times 2)$. Use the associative property to rewrite this expression.

_____

4. Ms. Smithson asks Claire to write an equation that shows "x less than 32 equals 15." Translate the phrase into an algebraic equation.

_____

5. What is the value of *n* in the equation below?

$$n - 5 = 6$$

$n =$ _____

6. Claire must earn 55 extra credit points to get an A in math. She has earned 30 points so far. Write an inequality to represent the amount of points, *p*, that Claire still needs to earn.

_____

Check What You Learned

Preparing for Algebra

Read the problem carefully and solve. Show your work under each question.

Claire decides to stay after school and help Ms. Smithson organize her classroom. Ms. Smithson asks Claire to draw a number line on the board and label some points for tomorrow's class. Claire draws the number line below.

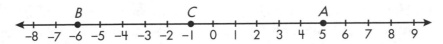

1. What integer does the letter *C* represent on Claire's number line?

   _____

2. Use > or < to compare the values of *A* and *B* on Claire's number line.

   5 _____ −6

3. Claire adds the values of the two numbers below to come up with a new point for her number line. What is the value of the expression below?

   $$5 + (-2)$$

   _____

4. Claire adds the values of the two numbers below to come up with a new point for her number line. What is the value of the expression below?

   $$-9 + 9$$

   _____

5. Claire organizes the books on Ms. Smithson's bookshelves. There are 3^3 books. Write this power as a product of factors.

   _____

6. Ms. Smithson also wants Claire to draw a grid and label point *A* on the grid for tomorrow's class. Plot point *A* at (6, 1) on the grid below.

   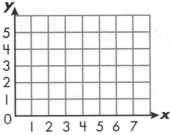

Final Test Chapters 1–13

Read the problem carefully and solve. Show your work under each question.

Michelle owns a farm stand. She is low on fruit and plans to order more. She decides to look at her sales from last month to see how much fruit she needs to order.

---

1. Michelle charges $2.83 for 1 pound of grapes. She sold 18.5 pounds of grapes last month. How much money did Michelle make in grape sales last month?

   _____

2. Last month, Michelle sold $12\frac{2}{3}$ pounds of red peppers. She sold $10\frac{1}{4}$ pounds of green peppers. How many more pounds of red peppers did she sell than green peppers?

   _____ lb.

3. Michelle charges $3.00 per pound for strawberries. Michelle made $108.00 in strawberry sales last month. How many pounds of strawberries did she sell?

   _____ lb.

4. Michelle looks at the total sales of grapefruit and watermelons from last month. She made $725.13 in grapefruit sales and $317.79 in watermelon sales. How much more money did she make from grapefruit sales than from watermelon sales?

   _____

5. Last month, Michelle had an apple sale. She sold bags of apples in two sizes. The small bag of apples weighed $2\frac{2}{3}$ pounds. The large bag of apples weighed $2\frac{3}{4}$ times more than the small bag. How much did the large bag of apples weigh?

   _____ lb.

6. Michelle has $5\frac{1}{4}$ pounds of raspberries left on her shelves. She wants to evenly divide them into containers that hold $2\frac{1}{3}$ pounds each. How many containers will she fill?

   _____ containers

Final Test Chapters 1-13

Read the problem carefully and solve. Show your work under each question.

Clark went to the West Side Mall to buy a shirt and a pair of pants. According to a map of the mall, there are 30 stores at the mall and 60% of these stores are clothing stores.

---

1. Write the percent of stores at the mall that sell clothing as a fraction in simplest form.

   _____

4. Clark buys a shirt that is 15% off. What is the discount on the shirt if the shirt originally costs $8?

   _____

2. How many clothing stores are at the West Side Mall?

   _____

5. Clark buys 2 pairs of pants. Each pair of pants costs $28.75. How much altogether do the 2 pairs of pants cost?

   _____

3. One of the clothing stores has a sale on shirts. Every shirt in the store is 15% off. How can this percent be written as a decimal?

   _____

6. Clark puts the clothes he bought into one bag. The total weight of the clothes is 5 pounds. How many ounces do the clothes weigh?

   _____ oz.

Spectrum Word Problems
Grade 6

Final Test
Chapters 1-13
109

CHAPTERS 1-13 FINAL TEST

Final Test Chapters 1–13

Read the problem carefully and solve. Show your work under each question.

Juan's school started a recycling project. Every homeroom in the school collected cans for 1 week. Homeroom teachers kept track of how many cans their students collected each day.

---

1. The line graph below shows the results for Ms. Rosetti's and Mr. Marsh's homerooms. Whose homeroom collected the most cans?

Results of Recycling Project

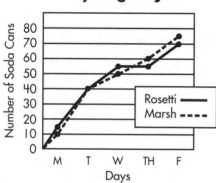

_____

2. Juan brought in the following number of cans each day during the week: 3, 2, 6, 2, and 7. What is the median of this data?

_____

3. The data set below shows the total number of cans brought in by each homeroom in the sixth grade. Draw a stem-and-leaf plot for this data.

85, 61, 76, 89, 54, 66

4. The circle graph below shows the different types of cans collected by the students in Mr. Monroe's class. The students in his class recycled a total of 80 cans. How many cans of soup did they recycle?

Types of Cans Recycled

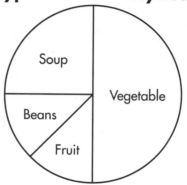

_____

5. Juan's friend Maria brought in a bag of 10 empty cans. Two of the empty cans are dented. If Juan reaches into the bag without looking, what is the probability of selecting a dented can?

_____

6. The data set below shows the total number of cans collected by each homeroom in the third grade. Using the number line below, draw a box-and-whisker plot for this data set.

10, 25, 30, 35, 40, 40, 45

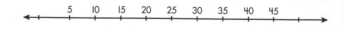

Final Test Chapters 1–13

Read the problem carefully and solve. Show your work under each question.

Jamal makes a design for a new park. The park will have a bricked area with picnic tables, gardens, and walking paths. He draws and labels a blueprint of the picnic area on a coordinate grid for the construction workers. He also draws a map of the park showing the gardens and the walking paths.

1. Jamal draws a blueprint of the picnic area on the grid below. He plots and labels the four points shown on the grid. Then, he connects the points with straight lines. What ordered pair represents point A?

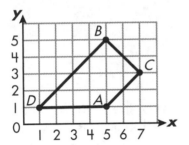

_____

2. Look at the drawing of the picnic area above. What is the name of this quadrilateral?

_____

3. Jamal wants to cover part of the picnic area with a roof. The roof is shaped like the solid figure below. How many faces does it have?

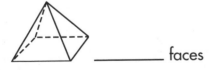

_____ faces

4. Jamal adds a circular garden to the map of the park. He will plant bushes on part of the garden and flowers on the other part. He draws a line segment in the circle below to show the two sides of the garden. Identify this line segment as a radius, chord, or diameter.

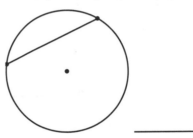

_____

5. Jamal draws straight lines on the map to represent two walking paths that intersect. This intersection forms two supplementary angles. He labels these two supplementary angles, ∠L and ∠M. The measure of ∠L is 138°. What is the measure of ∠M?

_____

6. Jamal draws another garden in the shape of the triangle shown below. Identify this triangle as acute, right, or obtuse.

_____

Final Test Chapters 1–13

Read the problem carefully and solve. Show your work under each question.

Jamal continues to plan for a new park. He wants to add a fountain in the middle of the park and more gardens near the entrance. He also orders some of the supplies he needs for the park.

---

1. Jamal plans to make a garden near the entrance of the park. It will be in the shape of a right triangle. The measurements of the garden are shown below. What is the perimeter of the garden? What is the area of the garden?

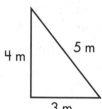

4 m 5 m 3 m

The perimeter of the garden is _____ meters.

The area of the garden is _____ square meters.

2. Jamal wants the fountain to be in a rectangular-shaped pool. The length of the pool will be 27 feet. The width of the pool will be 16 feet. Jamal wants the pool to be 4 feet deep. What will be the volume of the pool?

_____ cu. ft.

3. The length of the pool will be 27 feet. How long is the pool in yards?

_____ yd.

4. Jamal plans to use crushed stones on some of the walking paths. One bag of crushed stones he orders weighs 50 kilograms. What is this weight in grams?

_____ g

5. The length of the path from the picnic area to the fountain is 15 yards. Jamal needs to find this length in meters. To convert yards to meters, multiply by 0.914. What is the length of the path in meters?

_____ m

6. Jamal needs to paint the new picnic tables. He orders 6 gallons of paint. How many quarts are equal to 6 gallons?

_____ qt.

Final Test Chapters 1–13

Read the problem carefully and solve. Show your work under each question.

Tina wrote the ages of her family members as expressions and equations. She wants to find the ages of her brother, sister, mother, father, and grandmother.

1. Tina wrote her brother's age as the expression shown below. How old is her brother?

$$20 - 3 \times 3$$

_____ years old

4. Tina wrote the equation shown below to show her sister's age s. Solve the equation.

$$s \times 3 = 18$$

$s = $ _____

2. Tina wrote her father's age as the expression shown below. Use the distributive property to write an equivalent expression.

$$6 \times 4 + 6 \times 2$$

_____

5. Tina wrote her grandmother's age as g^3. If $g = 4$, how old is Tina's grandmother?

_____ years old

6. Tina wrote her own age as the expression shown below. How old is Tina?

$$-1 + (9)$$

_____ years old

3. Tina wrote the equation below to represent her mother's age. The variable m is equal to her mother's age. Solve the equation.

$$m - 14 = 20$$

$m = $ _____

Spectrum Word Problems
Grade 6

Final Test
Chapters 1–13

113

CHAPTERS 1–13 FINAL TEST

Scoring Record for Posttests, Mid-Test, and Final Test

Chapter Posttest	Your Score	Performance			
		Excellent	Very Good	Fair	Needs Improvement
1	____ of 6	6	5	3–4	2 or fewer
2	____ of 6	6	5	3–4	2 or fewer
3	____ of 6	6	5	3–4	2 or fewer
4	____ of 6	6	5	3–4	2 or fewer
5	____ of 6	6	5	3–4	2 or fewer
6	____ of 6	6	5	3–4	2 or fewer
7	____ of 6	6	5	3–4	2 or fewer
8	____ of 6	6	5	3–4	2 or fewer
9	____ of 6	6	5	3–4	2 or fewer
10	____ of 6	6	5	3–4	2 or fewer
11	____ of 12	11–12	9–10	7–8	6 or fewer
12	____ of 6	6	5	3–4	2 or fewer
13	____ of 12	11–12	9–10	7–8	6 or fewer
Mid-Test	____ of 24	22–24	20–21	16–19	15 or fewer
Final Test	____ of 36	33–36	29–32	23–28	22 or fewer

Record your test score in the Your Score column. See where your score falls in the Performance columns. Your score is based on the total number of required responses. If your score is fair or needs improvement, review the chapter material.

Grade 6 Answers

Chapter 1

Pretest, page 1
1. 16,807
2. 212
3. 30,362
4. 15,000
5. 11,987
6. 65,142

Lesson 1.1, page 2
1. 261
2. 239
3. 325
4. 145
5. 372

Lesson 1.2, page 3
1. 60,000
2. 310,000
3. 309,437
4. 391,353
5. 36,000

Lesson 1.3, page 4
1. 30,116
2. 31,771
3. 36,340
4. 44,066
5. 78,820

Posttest, page 5
1. 18,978
2. 397
3. 52,223
4. 40,000
5. 17,459
6. 84,339

Chapter 2

Pretest, page 6
1. 26; 11
2. 23; 0
3. 360
4. 93
5. 89
6. 492,900

Lesson 2.1, page 7
1. 252
2. 9,744
3. 65
4. 4,636
5. 364
6. 1,040

Lesson 2.2, page 8
1. 414,720
2. 786,432
3. 1,290,240

Lesson 2.3, page 9
1. 19; 0
2. 91; 2
3. 5; 50
4. 1,031; 3
5. 48; 5

Lesson 2.4, page 10
1. 46
2. 40; 12
3. 225
4. 41
5. 31; 17

Lesson 2.5, page 11
1. 300
2. 8,000
3. 60
4. 50
5. 100,000

Posttest, page 12
1. 1,465
2. 1
3. 403
4. 1,622
5. 6,000
6. 1,000,000

Chapter 3

Pretest, page 13
1. 3; 2
2. $\frac{10}{15}; \frac{12}{15}$
3. $\frac{31}{8}$
4. $13\frac{2}{7}$
5. $\frac{186}{14}$
6. 3

Grade 6 Answers

Lesson 3.1, page 14
1. dimes
2. quarters
3. $2 \cdot 3 \cdot 5$
4. $2 \cdot 2 \cdot 2 \cdot 3 \cdot 3$

Lesson 3.2, page 15
1. 4
2. 2
3. $\frac{2}{9}$
4. $\frac{5}{24}$
5. $\frac{1}{4}$

Lesson 3.3, page 16
1. $\frac{6}{15}$; $\frac{9}{15}$
2. $\frac{7}{10}$; $\frac{6}{10}$
3. $\frac{35}{60} < \frac{36}{60}$
4. 60
5. Eartha

Lesson 3.4, page 17
1. $1\frac{3}{4}$
2. $8\frac{2}{5}$
3. $7\frac{1}{7}$
4. $2\frac{1}{3}$; no
5. $22\frac{1}{2}$; yes

Lesson 3.5, page 18
1. $\frac{6}{5}$
2. $\frac{5}{2}$
3. $\frac{57}{4}$
4. $\frac{30}{7}$; $\frac{13}{3}$
5. Almonds. With a common denominator, the amounts are $\frac{90}{21}$ and $\frac{91}{21}$.

Lesson 3.6, page 19
1. $4\frac{3}{5}$
2. $4\frac{3}{4}$
3. $3\frac{1}{3}$
4. $6\frac{1}{4}$
5. Tuesday

Posttest, page 20
1. 11
2. 60
3. $\frac{3}{4}$
4. $\frac{35}{6}$
5. $7\frac{3}{4}$
6. $\frac{31}{4}$

Chapter 4

Pretest, page 21
1. $\frac{1}{2}$
2. $1\frac{1}{4}$
3. $\frac{9}{40}$
4. $7\frac{1}{15}$
5. $1\frac{11}{15}$
6. $4\frac{31}{56}$

Lesson 4.1, page 22
1. $1\frac{3}{8}$
2. $1\frac{5}{12}$
3. $\frac{1}{2}$
4. $\frac{7}{10}$
5. $1\frac{11}{30}$

Lesson 4.2, page 23
1. $5\frac{1}{6}$
2. $5\frac{5}{6}$
3. $4\frac{34}{45}$
4. $7\frac{8}{9}$
5. $9\frac{8}{15}$

Lesson 4.3, page 24
1. $1\frac{1}{4}$
2. $3\frac{1}{3}$
3. $3\frac{1}{60}$
4. $\frac{11}{12}$
5. $2\frac{1}{10}$

Grade 6 Answers

Posttest, page 25

1. $1\frac{1}{7}$
2. $\frac{5}{14}$
3. $4\frac{5}{12}$
4. $1\frac{11}{30}$
5. $7\frac{7}{12}$
6. $1\frac{25}{28}$

Chapter 5

Pretest, page 26

1. $\frac{1}{2}$
2. $\frac{2}{9}$
3. $4\frac{3}{8}$
4. 3
5. $7\frac{1}{2}$
6. $1\frac{1}{10}$

Lesson 5.1, page 27

1. 7
2. $3\frac{1}{3}$
3. $3\frac{3}{4}$
4. $4\frac{1}{5}$
5. 5

Lesson 5.2, page 28

1. $11\frac{11}{12}$
2. $12\frac{3}{8}$
3. $20\frac{5}{8}$
4. $5\frac{2}{5}$
5. $10\frac{1}{2}$

Lesson 5.3, page 29

1. $\frac{3}{2}$
2. $\frac{1}{6}$
3. $\frac{1}{8}$
4. $\frac{3}{16}$
5. $\frac{3}{10}$

Lesson 5.4, page 30

1. $2\frac{1}{4}$
2. $1\frac{1}{5}$
3. $1\frac{1}{3}$
4. $3\frac{1}{2}$
5. $2\frac{3}{16}$

Lesson 5.5, page 31

1. $2\frac{1}{2}$
2. $2\frac{19}{28}$
3. $1\frac{1}{4}$
4. 2
5. $1\frac{3}{5}$

Posttest, page 32

1. $\frac{1}{6}$
2. $2\frac{2}{5}$
3. $\frac{1}{10}$
4. $8\frac{1}{3}$
5. $12\frac{2}{3}$
6. $\frac{3}{4}$

Chapter 6

Pretest, page 33

1. 42.81 cm > 42.08 cm
2. Forty-two and eight hundredths
3. 4.25
4. $\frac{6}{25}$
5. 2.18
6. $261.47

Lesson 6.1, page 34

1. 1
2. 7
3. one hundred seventy-eight thousandths
4. thirty-four hundredths
5. 1.308

Lesson 6.2, page 35

1. 0.6
2. 1.75
3. 0.240
4. 3.80
5. 3.800

Grade 6 Answers

Lesson 6.3, page 36

1. $2\frac{3}{20}$
2. $1\frac{7}{100}$
3. $\frac{21}{50}$
4. $\frac{9}{40}$
5. $1\frac{7}{25}$

Lesson 6.4, page 37

1. 3.12 cm > 3.02 cm
2. 4.92 cm < 5.3 cm
3. 8.12 cm < 8.13 cm
4. 4.96, 5.06, 5.61, 6.01
5. 0.073 m > 0.070 m

Lesson 6.5, page 38

1. $97.09
2. $11.04
3. $135.05
4. No, she will not have enough. She will be over by $10.07.
5. $2,856.57

Posttest, page 39

1. 16.57 < 16.75
2. sixteen and fifty-seven hundredths
3. 2.2
4. $\frac{17}{25}$
5. 0.894
6. $49.76

Mid-Test

Page 40

1. 122
2. 381
3. 82,946
4. 15
5. 208
6. 20

Page 41

1. 4
2. $\frac{19}{28}; \frac{19}{28}$
3. $2\frac{1}{3}$
4. $1\frac{2}{7}$
5. $1\frac{13}{30}$
6. $6\frac{5}{63}$

Page 42

1. $\frac{5}{12}$
2. $1\frac{1}{2}$
3. $2\frac{7}{10}$
4. 30
5. $3\frac{3}{5}$
6. $9\frac{1}{15}$

Page 43

1. one and sixty-three hundredths
2. $\frac{6}{25}$
3. 2.3
4. <
5. 1.39
6. $8.16

Chapter 7

Pretest, page 44

1. 21.5
2. $28.35
3. 81.7
4. 3
5. 21
6. 12

Lesson 7.1, page 45

1. 15.80
2. 9.425
3. $10.32
4. $5.91
5. $1,135.55

Lesson 7.2, page 46

1. 88
2. 400
3. 7
4. 2,250
5. 4,000

Lesson 7.3, page 47

1. $7.10
2. 15
3. $45.50
4. 45
5. $52.23

Grade 6 Answers

Posttest, page 48
1. $9.15
2. 6.226
3. 0.49
4. 33
5. 24
6. $8.45

Chapter 8

Pretest, page 49
1. 0.14
2. 60%
3. 0.65
4. 24
5. $1\frac{1}{4}$
6. 6.51

Lesson 8.1, page 50
1. $\frac{3}{10}$
2. 52%
3. $\frac{9}{20}$
4. $\frac{19}{50}$
5. 65%

Lesson 8.2, page 51
1. 0.32
2. 13%
3. 0.045
4. 0.78
5. 27%

Lesson 8.3, page 52
1. $1\frac{24}{25}$
2. $1\frac{1}{5}$
3. $2\frac{11}{20}$
4. $19\frac{1}{2}$
5. $18\frac{18}{25}$

Lesson 8.4, page 53
1. 3.19
2. 10.4
3. 9
4. 38
5. 64

Lesson 8.5, page 54
1. 16:3
2. 2
3. 4:18
4. 20
5. 8:6

Lesson 8.6, page 55
1. $24, $30, $36
2. $42, $48, $54
3. dots at (1, 6), (2, 12), (3, 18), and (4, 24)
4. dots at (5, 30), (6, 36), (7, 42), (8, 48), and (9, 54)

Posttest, page 56
1. 0.22
2. 60%
3. 0.84
4. 10:15
5. $3\frac{9}{10}$
6. 3.36

Chapter 9

Pretest, page 57
1. 3
2. 10
3. 15
4. 2
5. 96
6. 336

Lesson 9.1, page 58
1. 84
2. 27
3. 0.5
4. 40
5. 5,280

Lesson 9.2, page 59
1. 4
2. 8
3. 100
4. 0.5
5. 128

Lesson 9.3, page 60
1. 8
2. 352
3. 960
4. 1.5
5. 5,000

Grade 6 Answers

Lesson 9.4, page 61
1. 26
2. 86
3. 40
4. 27.5
5. 10,800

Posttest, page 62
1. 36
2. 45
3. 54
4. 648
5. 18,000
6. 20

Chapter 10

Pretest, page 63
1. 200
2. 500
3. 0.5
4. 48
5. 80
6. 12.71

Lesson 10.1, page 64
1. 2,000
2. 60
3. 0.25
4. 0.324
5. 4,950

Lesson 10.2, page 65
1. 4,000
2. 0.5
3. 0.012
4. 5.253
5. 980

Lesson 10.3, page 66
1. 0.68
2. 1,600
3. 1.8
4. 590,000
5. 270

Lesson 10.4, page 67
1. 32
2. 64
3. 56
4. 160
5. 1,280

Lesson 10.5, page 68
1. 25.4
2. 1.89
3. 311.85
4. 236.59
5. 1.53

Posttest, page 69
1. 800
2. 0.12
3. 123
4. 2,700
5. 60
6. 1.83

Chapter 11

Pretest, page 70
1. 10
2. Mr. Moore
3. 4
4. 5
5.

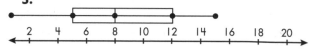

6. $\frac{5}{23}$

Pretest, page 71
1. Basketball
2. Hockey and Swimming
3.

	math club
basketball	newspaper
	student council
volleyball	math club
	newspaper
	student council
swimming	math club
	newspaper
	student council
hockey	math club
	newspaper
	student council

12
4. $\frac{1}{6}$
5. 16
6.

Stem	Leaves
1	4 6 9
2	4
3	0

Grade 6 Answers

Lesson 11.1, page 72
1. Wednesday
2. Jordan
3. 7
4. 8
5. 23

Lesson 11.2, page 73
1. Tyrone
2. Wednesday
3. Wednesday; Friday
4. Tuesday
5. $195

Lesson 11.3, page 74
1. Apple
2. 5
3. 10
4. $160
5. $60

Lesson 11.4, page 75
1. 5.5
2. 5; 12
3. 5.5
4. 6.4; 6
   5; 14
5. The mean changed the most. Last year's mean is 1.2 less than this year's mean.

Lesson 11.5, page 76

1.
Stem	Leaves
6	8
7	1 9
8	1 5 8
9	2 3

2.
Stem	Leaves
6	5 8
8	1 1 4
9	2 2 5

3.
Stem	Leaves
7	0 5 8 8
8	0 6 7 8

4.
Stem	Leaves
1	4 6 9
2	4
3	0

5. Raul

Lesson 11.6, page 77
1. 25
2. 15
3. 30
4.

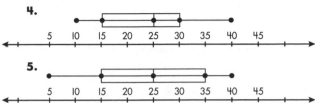

5.

Lesson 11.7, page 78
1. $\frac{1}{3}$
2. heads — heads, tails; tails — heads, tails
3. $\frac{1}{4}$
4. 1 — 1, 2, 3; 2 — 1, 2, 3; 3 — 1, 2, 3
5. $\frac{4}{9}$

Posttest, page 79
1. 20
2. Lucas
3. 40
4. 30
5.

6. $\frac{1}{5}$

Posttest, page 80
1. Blue
2. Green
3. red — red, blue, green; blue — red, blue, green; green — red, blue, green
4. $\frac{2}{9}$
5. 22
6.
Stem	Leaves
1	4 7
2	0 6
3	3

Grade 6 Answers

Chapter 12

Pretest, page 81
1. square pyramid; 5; 5
2. right
3.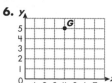
   $\overset{\bullet}{A} \qquad \overset{\bullet}{B}\!\!\rightarrow$
4. rhombus; not congruent
5. diameter

Lesson 12.1, page 82
1. $\overset{\bullet}{C} \qquad \overset{\bullet}{D}$
2. ray; $\overrightarrow{MN}$
3.
   L
   $J \qquad K$
4. RQP or PQR; obtuse; 110°
5. ABC or CBA; acute; 40°

Lesson 12.2, page 83
1. vertical
2. supplementary
3. 55°
4. 56°
5. 50°

Lesson 12.3, page 84
1. obtuse
2. 4.25 cm^2
3. right
4. 4.725 cm^2
5. acute

Lesson 12.4, page 85
1. A, D, G
2. C, F
3. $289\frac{1}{3}$ in^3
4. kite; not congruent
5. congruent

Lesson 12.5, page 86
1. Plot school at (−1, 1).
   Plot office at (4, 1).
   Plot park at (4, −4).
2. triangle
3. (−1, 1) to (4, 1)
4. 5
5. 12.5

Lesson 12.6, page 87
1. $\overline{RV}$ or $\overline{VR}$
2. $\overline{SR}, \overline{ST}, \overline{SV}$ or $\overline{RS}, \overline{TS}, \overline{VS}$
3. $\overline{WV}$ or $\overline{VW}$
4. S
5. chord

Lesson 12.7, page 88
1. rectangular solid; 8 vertices
2. square pyramid; triangular solid
3. 2 more
4. cylinder
5. cone

Posttest, page 89
1. triangular pyramid; 4; 4
2. obtuse
3. $\overset{\bullet}{R} \qquad \overset{\bullet}{S}$
4. radius
5. trapezoid; congruent
6. complementary; 52°

Chapter 13

Pretest, page 90
1. 6
2. 6 × (1 + 2)
3. 8 + (3 + 4)
4. 5 × n = 25
5. 12
6. 24

Pretest, page 91
1. 7 × 7 × 7 × 7
2. <
3. 6, −3, −2, 2, 5
4. 3
5. −8
6.
   y
   5
   4
   3
   2
   1
   0 1 2 3 4 5 6 7   x

Lesson 13.1, page 92
1. division
2. addition
3. 9
4. 8
5. 2

Grade 6 Answers

Lesson 13.2, page 93
1. 3×4
2. $2 + (5 + 4)$
3. $(4 \times 6) + (4 \times 2)$
4. $1 \times (4 \times 2)$
5. $5 \times (1 + 6)$

Lesson 13.3, page 94
1. expression
2. equation
3. $7; b$
4. $x + 7$
5. $y \times 12 = 84$

Lesson 13.4, page 95
1. subtraction
2. addition
3. 8
4. 24
5. 50

Lesson 13.5, page 96
1. multiplication
2. division
3. 24
4. 8
5. 20

Lesson 13.6, page 97
1. $2p + 3$
2. $28 + 0.35t$
3. $15h + 20 = 85$
4. $2c - 4 = s$
5. $\$5 + n = t$
6. possible answer: Sara spent $15 at a craft store. She bought 1 notebook for $3. She bought 2 paintbrushes for x dollars. If each paintbrush cost the same, what was the cost of 1 brush?

Lesson 13.7, page 98
1. $m \geq \$80$
2.
$\$70 \quad \$75 \quad \$80 \quad \$85 \quad \$90$
3. $250 > y$
4.
$0 \quad 50 \quad 100 \quad 150 \quad 200 \quad 250$
5. $x \geq 6$

Lesson 13.8, page 99
1. 4×10^3
2. 4×10^2
3. 12×12
4. 5^4
5. 64

Lesson 13.9, page 100
1. 27 or $|-27|$
2. 150 or $|-150|$
3. Sam
4. 12 or $|-12|$
5. 14 or $|-14|$
6. 40 or $|-40|$

Lesson 13.10, page 101
1. 1
2. 3
3. $>$
4. $<$
5. $-7, -3, 0, 5$

Lesson 13.11, page 102
1. 8
2. -7
3. 3
4. -5
5. -10

Lesson 13.12, page 103
1. $-10, +10$; yes
2. yes
3. -18
4. 400
5. yes
6. plot dots at -20 and 20

Lesson 13.13, page 104
1. D
2. K
3. $(5, 5)$
4. $(9, 4)$
5.

Spectrum Word Problems
Grade 6

Answer Key

123

Grade 6 Answers

Lesson 13.14, page 105

1. Quadrant II
2. (7, −4)
3. C
4.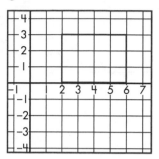
5. graph point K at (−3, 9)
6. 4

Posttest, page 106

1. 22
2. (4 × 5) + (4 × 9)
3. (4 × 3) × 2
4. 32 − x = 15
5. 11
6. $p \geq 25$

Posttest, page 107

1. −1
2. >
3. 3
4. 0
5. 3 3 3 3 3
6.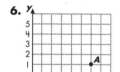

Final Test

Page 108

1. $52.36
2. $\frac{5}{12}$
3. 36
4. $407.34
5. $7\frac{1}{3}$
6. $2\frac{1}{4}$

Page 109

1. $\frac{3}{5}$
2. 18
3. 0.15
4. $1.20
5. $57.50
6. 80

Page 110

1. Mr. Marsh
2. 3
3.

Stem	Leaves
5	4
6	1 6
7	6
8	5 9

4. 20
5. $\frac{1}{5}$
6.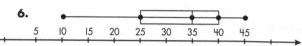

Page 111

1. (5,1)
2. trapezoid
3. 5
4. chord
5. 42°
6. acute

Page 112

1. 12; 6
2. 1,728
3. 9
4. 50,000
5. 13.71
6. 24

Page 113

1. 11
2. 6 × (4 + 2)
3. 34
4. 6
5. 64
6. 8